CHRISTIANITY IN A NUTSHELL!

Learn to Fight the Devil, Get Eternal Life, and Be Free from Sin.

B.B. WATTS

WESTBOW
PRESS®
A DIVISION OF THOMAS NELSON
& ZONDERVAN

WestBow Press books may be ordered through booksellers or by contacting:

WestBow Press
A Division of Thomas Nelson & Zondervan
1663 Liberty Drive
Bloomington, IN 47403
www.westbowpress.com
1 (866) 928-1240

Scripture taken from the King James Version of the Bible.

ISBN: 978-1-9736-8497-8 (sc)
ISBN: 978-1-9736-8499-2 (hc)
ISBN: 978-1-9736-8498-5 (e)

Library of Congress Control Number: 2020902475

Print information available on the last page.

WestBow Press rev. date: 07/09/2020

How to be equipped against the devil's schemes on planet Earth, get eternal life after death, and have freedom from being a slave to sin.

To God and every hero of the faith I have learned about and gleaned wisdom from.

Contents

Step 1: Get Saved

Saved from what, you ask? This saves you from your sins (John 8:24; 1 John 1:9) on planet Earth and God's coming wrath (Ephesians 2:1–10). And it saves you from hell after you die so you live on (John 3:16). It gives you eternal life. Apply or do what Romans says to do here, and you will be saved!

○ For God so loved the world, that he gave his only begotten Son, that whosoever believeth in him should not perish, but have everlasting life. (John 3:16)

○ That if thou shalt confess with thy mouth the Lord Jesus, and shalt believe in thine heart that God hath raised him from the dead, thou shalt be saved. For with the heart man believeth unto righteousness; and with the mouth confession is made unto salvation. . . . For whosoever shall call upon the name of the Lord shall be saved. (Romans 10:9–10, 13)

Response

Awesome! You have now, just made yourself a fighter for good on planet Earth, something God can only equip you with. Not to mention this is the most important thing you will ever do next to getting married. The only time this doesn't work is if you have already denounced your faith. There is no going back! Please don't ever do that for you, God, your family, friends, and future generations. If you have already received your salvation, you don't need to do it again.

Step 2: Get Baptized

It is your first command.

- He that believeth and is baptized shall be saved; but he that believeth not shall be damned. (Mark 16:16)
- Then Peter said unto them, repent, and be baptized every one of you in the name of Jesus Christ for the remission of sins, and ye shall receive the gift of the Holy Ghost. (Acts 2:38)
- Can any man forbid water, that these should not be baptized, which have received the Holy Ghost as well as we? (Acts 10:47)
- And Crispus, the chief ruler of the synagogue, believed on the Lord with all his house; and many of the Corinthians hearing believed, and were baptized. (Acts 18:8)
- And now why tarriest thou? Arise, and be baptized, and wash away thy sins, calling on the name of the Lord. (Acts 22:16)
- Go ye therefore, and teach all nations, baptizing them in the name of the Father, and of the Son, and of the Holy Ghost. (Matthew 28:19)

Summary

It says to get saved and be baptized. A local pastor should be able to do this for you, and like it says, you should be baptized in the name of the Father, Son, and the Holy Spirit.

Step 3: Get the Holy Spirit

- But when they shall lead you, and deliver you up, take no thought beforehand what ye shall speak, neither do ye premeditate: but whatsoever shall be given you in that hour, that speak ye: for it is not ye that speak, but the Holy Ghost. (Mark 13:11)
- If ye then, being evil, know how to give good gifts unto your children: how much more shall your heavenly Father give the Holy Spirit to them that ask him? (Luke 11:13)
- And when they bring you unto the synagogues and unto magistrates, and powers, take ye no thought how or what thing ye shall say: For the Holy Ghost shall teach you in the same hour what ye ought to say. (Luke 12:11–12)
- And I will pray the Father, and he shall give you another Comforter, that he may abide with you forever. (John 14:16)
- But the Comforter, which is the Holy Ghost, whom the Father will send in my name, he shall teach you all things, and bring all things to your remembrance, whatsoever I have said unto to you. (John 14:26)
- But when the Comforter is come, whom I will send unto you from the Father, even the Spirit of truth, which proceedeth from the Father, he shall testify of me. (John 15:26)
- Nevertheless I tell you the truth: It is expedient for you that I go away: for if I go not away, the Comforter will not come unto you; but if I depart, I will send him unto you. . . . Howbeit when he, the Spirit of truth is come, he will guide you into all truth: for he shall not speak of himself: but whatsoever he shall hear, that shall he speak: and he will show you things to come. (John 16:7, 13)

- But ye shall receive power, after that the Holy Ghost is come upon you: and ye shall be witnesses unto me both in Jerusalem, and in all Judea, and in Samaria, and unto the uttermost part of the earth. (Acts 1:8)
- And they were all filled with the Holy Ghost, and began to speak with other tongues, as the Spirit gave them utterance. . . . Then Peter said unto them, Repent and be baptized every one of you in the name of Jesus Christ for the remission of sins, and ye shall receive the gift of the Holy Ghost. (Acts 2:4, 38)
- Then Peter, filled with the Holy Ghost, said unto them, Ye rulers of the people, and elders of Israel. . . . And when they had prayed, the place was shaken where they were assembled together: and they were all filled with the Holy Ghost, and they spake the word of God with boldness. (Acts 4:8, 31)
- And we are his witnesses of these things, and so is also the Holy Ghost, whom God hath given to them that obey him. (Acts 5:32)
- Who, when they were come down, prayed for them, that they might receive the Holy Ghost. . . . Then laid they their hands on them, and they received the Holy Ghost. (Acts 8:15, 17)
- To him give all the prophets witness, that through his name whosoever believeth in him shall receive remission of sins. While Peter yet spake these words, the Holy Ghost fell on all them which heard the word. And they of the circumcision which believed were astonished, as many as came with Peter, because that on the Gentiles also was poured out the gift of the Holy Ghost. (Acts 10:43–45)
- And as I began to speak the Holy Ghost fell on them, as on us at the beginning. (Acts 11:15)
- As they ministered to the Lord, and fasted, the Holy Ghost said, Separate me Barnabas and Saul for the work whereunto I have called them. . . . And the disciples were filled with joy, and with the Holy Ghost. (Acts 13:2, 52)
- And God, which knoweth the hearts, bare them witness, giving them the Holy Ghost, even as he did unto us. . . . For it seemed good to the Holy Ghost, and to us, to lay upon you no greater burden than these necessary things. (Acts 15:8, 28)
- And when Paul had laid his hands upon them, the Holy Ghost came on them: and they spake with tongues and prophesied. (Acts 19:6)

- And hope maketh not ashamed; because the love of God is shed abroad in our hearts by the Holy Ghost which is given unto us. (Romans 5:5)
- Now the God of hope fill you with all joy and peace in believing, that ye may abound in hope, through the power of the Holy Ghost. . . . That I should be the minister of Jesus Christ to the Gentiles, ministering the gospel of God, that the offering up of the Gentiles might be acceptable, being sanctified by the Holy Ghost. (Romans 15:13, 16)
- What: know ye not that your body is the temple of the Holy Ghost which is in you, which ye have of God, and ye are not your own? (1 Corinthians 6:19)
- Wherefore I give you to understand, that no man speaking by the Spirit of God calleth Jesus accursed: and that no man can say that Jesus is the Lord, but by the Holy Ghost. (1 Corinthians 12:3)
- By pureness, by knowledge, by longsuffering, by kindness, by the Holy Ghost, by love unfeigned. (2 Corinthians 6:6)
- The grace of the Lord Jesus Christ, and the love of God, and the communion of the Holy Ghost be with you all. Amen. (2 Corinthians 13:14)
- In whom ye also trusted, after that he heard the word of truth the gospel of your salvation in whom also after that ye believed, ye were sealed with the Holy Spirit of promise. Which is the earnest of our inheritance until the redemption of the purchased possession, unto the praise of his glory. (Ephesians 1:13–14)
- And grieve not the Holy Spirit of God, where by ye are sealed unto the day of redemption. (Ephesians 4:30)
- For our gospel came not unto you in word only, but also in power, and in the Holy Ghost, and in much assurance: as ye know what manner of men we were among you for your sake. And ye became followers of us, and of the Lord, having received the word in much affliction, with joy of the Holy Ghost. (1 Thessalonians 1:5–6)
- That good thing which was committed unto thee keep by the Holy Ghost which dwelleth in us. (2 Timothy 1:14)
- But after that the kindness and love of God our Savior toward man appeared, Not by works of righteousness which we have done, but according to his mercy he saved us, by the washing of regeneration,

and renewing of the Holy Ghost; Which he shed on us abundantly through Jesus Christ our Savior. (Titus 3:4–6)

- God also bearing them witness, both with signs and wonders, and divers miracles, and gifts of the Holy Ghost, according to his own will? (Hebrews 2:4)
- For by one offering he hath perfected forever them that are sanctified. Where of the Holy Ghost also is a witness to us: for after that he had said before, This is the covenant that I will make with them after those days, saith the Lord, I will put my laws into their hearts, and in their minds will I write them. (Hebrews 10:14–16)
- But ye, beloved, building up yourself on your most holy faith, praying in the Holy Ghost. (Jude 1:20)
- And I was with you in weakness, and in fear, and in much trembling. And my speech and my preaching was not with enticing words of man's wisdom, but in demonstration of the Spirit and of power: That your faith should not stand in the wisdom of men, but in the power of God. (1 Corinthians 2:3–5)
- For this cause we also, since the day we heard it, do not cease to pray for you, and to desire that ye might be filled with knowledge of his will in all wisdom and spiritual understanding. (Colossians 1:9)
- Quench not the Spirit. (1 Thessalonians 5:19)
- But we are bound to give thanks always to God for you, brethren beloved of the Lord, because God hath from the beginning chosen you to salvation through sanctification of the Spirit and belief of the truth. (2 Thessalonians 2:13)
- For God hath not given us the spirit of fear; but of power, and of love, and of a sound mind. (2 Timothy 1:7)
- How much more shall the blood of Christ, who through the eternal Spirit offered himself with out spot to God, purge your conscience from dead works to serve the living God. (Hebrews 9:14)
- Elect according to the foreknowledge of God the Father, through sanctification of the Spirit, unto obedience and sprinkling of the blood of Jesus Christ: Grace unto you, and peace, be multiplied. (1 Peter 1:2)
- This is he that came by water and blood, even Jesus Christ; not by water only, but by water and blood. And it is the Spirit that beareth witness, because the Spirit is truth. (1 John 5:6)

- But ye, beloved, building up yourselves on your holy faith, praying in the Holy Ghost. (Jude 1:20)
- For what man knoweth the things of a man, save the spirit of man which is in him? Even so the things of God knoweth no man but the Spirit of God. (1 Corinthians 2:11)
- Endeavoring to keep the unity of the Spirit in the bond of peace. There is one body, and one Spirit, even as ye are called in one hope of your calling: One Lord, one faith, one baptism. (Ephesians 4:3–5)
- Only let your conversation be as it becometh the gospel of Christ: that whether I come and see you, or else be absent, I may hear of your affairs, that ye stand fast in one spirit, with one mind striving together for the faith of the gospel. (Philippians 1:27)
- For as the body is one, and hath many members, and all the members of that one body, being many, are one body: so also is Christ. For by one Spirit are we all baptized into one body, whether we be Jews or Gentiles, whether we be bond or free: and have been all made to drink into one Spirit. For the body is not one member, but many. (1 Corinthians 12:12–14)

Summary

Also called the Spirit of Truth and Advocate, according to Jesus, you get the Holy Spirit by asking for the Holy Spirit. It is by the Holy Spirit that power, sanctification, joy, wisdom, understanding, love, self-discipline, and sealing are brought to your faith. There is only one Spirit, and it can come on a person through laying on of hands and on an audience as the truth is spoken to them. The Holy Spirit will speak for you when you testify of your faith.

Step 4: Things You Believe as a Christian

God created the earth in six days, and on the seventh day, He rested. He also created man in His image.

○ In the beginning God created the heaven and the earth. And the earth was without form, and void: and darkness was upon the face of the deep. And the Spirit of God moved upon the face of the waters. And God said, Let there be light and there was light. And God saw the light, that it was good: and God divided the light from the darkness. And God called the light Day and the darkness he called Night. And the evening and the morning were the first day. And God said, let there be a firmament in the midst of the waters, and let it divide the waters from the waters. And God made the firmament, and divided the waters which were under the firmament from the waters which were above the firmament: and it was so. And God called the firmament Heaven. And the evening and the morning were the second day. And God said, let the waters under the heaven be gathered together unto one place, and let the dry land appear: and it was so. And God called the dry land Earth; and the gathering together of the waters called he Seas: and God saw that it was good. And God said, let the earth bring forth grass, the herb yielding seed, and the fruit tree yielding fruit after his kind, whose seed is in itself, upon the earth: and it was so. And the earth brought forth grass, and herb yielding seed after his kind, and the tree yielding fruit, whose seed was in itself, after his kind: and God saw that it was good. And the evening and the morning were the third day. And God said, Let there be lights in the firmament of the heaven to divide the day from the night: and let them be for signs, and for seasons, and for days, and years: And let them be for lights in the firmament of the heaven to give light upon the earth: and it was so. And God made two great lights: the greater light to rule the day, and the lesser light to rule the night; He made the stars also. And God set them in the firmament of the heaven to give light upon the earth, And to rule over the day and over the night, and to divide the light from the darkness: and God saw that it was good. And the evening and the morning were the fourth day. And God said, Let the waters bring forth abundantly the moving creature that hath life, and fowl that may fly above the earth in the open firmament of heaven. And God created great whales, and every living creature that moveth, which the waters brought forth abundantly, after their kind, and every winged fowl after his kind: and God saw that it was good. And God blessed them, saying, Be fruitful, and multiply, and fill the waters in the seas, and let fowl multiply in the earth. And the evening and the morning were the fifth day. And God said, Let the earth bring forth the living creature after his kind, cattle, and creeping thing, and beast of the earth after his kind: and it was so. And God made the beast of earth after his kind, and cattle after their kind, and everything that creepeth upon the earth after his kind: and God saw that it was good. And God said, Let us make man in our images, after our likeness: and let them have dominion over the fish of the sea, and over the fowl of the air, and over the cattle, and over all the earth, and over every creeping thing that creepeth up on the earth. So God created man in his own image, in the image of God created he him: male and female created he them. And God blessed them, and God said unto them, Be fruitful, and multiply, and replenish the earth, and subdue it: and have dominion over the fish of the sea, and over the fowl of the air, and over every living thing that moveth upon the earth. And God said, Behold, I have given you every herb bearing seed, which is upon the face of all the earth, and every tree, in the which is the fruit of the tree yielding seed: to you it shall be for meat. And to every beast of the earth, and to every fowl of the air, and to everything that creepeth upon the earth, wherein there is life, I have given every green herb for meat: and it was so. And

God saw every thing that He had made, and, behold, it was very good. And the evening and the morning were the sixth day. (Genesis 1:1–31)

o Thus the heavens and the earth were finished and all the host of them. And on the seventh day God ended his work which he had made: and he rested on the seventh day from all his work which he had made. And God blessed the seventh day, and sanctified it: because that in it he had rested from all his work which God created and made. (Genesis 2:1–3)

o For in six days the Lord made heaven and earth, the sea, and all that in them is, and rested the seventh day; wherefore the Lord blessed the sabbath day, and hallowed it. (Exodus 20:11)

The genealogy from Adam to Jesus and from Jesus until now tells how old humans and the earth are.

o The book of the generation of Jesus Christ, the son of David, the son of Abraham. Abraham begat Isaac: and Isaac begat Jacob; and Jacob begat Judas and his brethren; And Judas begat Phares and Zara of Thamar; and Phares begat Esrom; and Esrom begat Aram; And Aram begat Aminadab; and Aminadab begat Naason; and Naason begat Salmon And Salmon begat Boaz of Rachab; and Boaz begat Obed of Ruth; and Obed begat Jesse: And Jesse begat David the king; and David the king begat Solomon of her that had been the wife of Urias: And Solomon begat Roboam; and Roboam begat Abia; and Abia begat Asa; And Asa begat Josaphat; and Jeoshaphat begat Joram; and Joram begat Ozias; And Ozias begat Joatham; and Joatham begat Achaz; and Achaz begat Ezekias; And Ezekias begat Manasses; and Manasses begat Amon; and Amon begat Josiah; And Josiah begat Jechoniah and his brethren and about the time they were carried away to Babylon; And after they were brought to Babylon, Jechoniah begat Salathiel; and Salathiel begat Zorobabel; And Zorobabel begat Abiud; and Abiud begat Eliakim; and Eliakim begat Azor; And Azor begat Sadoc; and Sadoc begat Achim; and Achim begat Eliud; And Eliud begat Eleazar; and Eleazar begat Matthan; and Matthan begat Jacob; And Jacob begat Joseph the husband of Mary, of whom was born Jesus, who is called Christ. So all the generation from Abraham to David until the carrying away into Babylon are fourteen generation; and from the carrying away into Babylon unto Christ are fourteen generations. (Matthew 1:1–17)

○ And Jesus himself began to be about thirty years of age, being (as was supposed) the son of Joseph, which was the son of Heli, which was the son of Matthat, which was the son of Levi, which was the son of Melchi, which was the son of Janna, which was the son of Joseph, which was the son of Mattathias, which was the son of Amos, which was the son of Naum, which was the son of Esli, which was the son of Nagge, Which was the son of Maath, which was the son of Mattathias, which was the son of Semei, which was the son of Joseph, which was the son of Juda, which was the son of Joanna, which was the son of Rhesa, which was the son of Zorobabel, which was the son of Salathiel, which was the son of Neri, which was the son of Melchi, which was the son of Addi, which was the son of Cosam, which was the son of Eldodam, which was the son of Er, which was the son of Jose, which was the son of Eliezer, which was the son of Jorim, which was the son of Matthat, which was the son of Levi, which was the son of Simeon, which was the son of Juda, which was the son of Joseph, which was the son of Jonan, which was the son of Eliakim, which was the son of Melea, which was the son of Menan, which was the son of Mattatha, which was the son of Nathan, which was the son of David, which was the son of Jesse, which was the son of Obed, which was the son of Boaz, which was the son of Salmon, which was the son of Naasson, which was the son of Aminadab, which was the son of Aram, which was the son of Esrom, which was the son of Phares, which was the son of Juda, which was the son of Jacob, which was the son of Isaac, which was the son of Abraham, which was the son of Thara, which was the son of Nachor, which was the son of Saruch, which was the son of Ragau, which was the son of Phalec, which was the son of Heber, which was the son of Sala, which was the son of Cainan, which was the son of Arphaxad, which was the son of Shem, which was the son of Noah, which was the son of Lamech, which was the son of Mathuselah, which was the son of Enoch, which was the son of Jared, which was the son of Maleleel, which was the son of Cainan, which was the son of Enos, which was the son of Seth, which was the son of Adam, which was the son of God. (Luke 3:23–38)

Response

I have heard two things:

1. The genealogy from Adam to Jesus is ten thousand years and from Jesus until now it has been two thousand years, making the earth twelve thousand years old.
2. The genealogy from Adam to David is two thousand years, from David to Jesus is two thousand years, and from Jesus until now it has been two thousand years, making the earth six thousand years old.

   Either way, the Bible says all of this takes place in a short amount of time in heaven; otherwise God wouldn't be able to bear all the pain and suffering people go through.

A thousand years is like a day to God in heaven.

○ For a thousand years in thy sight are but as yesterday when it is past, and as a watch in the night. (Psalm 90:4)
○ But, beloved, be not ignorant of this one thing, that one day is with the Lord as a thousand years, and a thousand years as one day. (2 Peter 3:8)

Response

So if it has been twelve thousand years here on earth, it has been twelve days to God in heaven. Or if it has been six thousand years here on earth, it has been six days to God in heaven.

Christ will return to earth and reign for a thousand years on earth.

○ And I saw thrones, and they sat upon them, and judgment was given unto them: and I saw the souls of them that were beheaded for the witness of Jesus, and for the word of God, and which had not worshiped the beast, neither his image, neither had received his mark upon their foreheads, or in their hands; and they lived and reigned with Christ a thousand years. But the rest of the dead lived not again until the thousand years were finished. This is the first resurrection. Blessed and holy is he that hath part in the first resurrection: on such the second death hath no power, but they shall be priests of God and of Christ, and shall reign with him a thousand years. (Revelation 20:4–7)

You believe there will be a new earth, a new heaven, and a New Jerusalem.

○ Nevertheless we, according to his promise, look for new heavens and a new earth, wherein dwelleth righteousness. (2 Peter 3:13)

○ And I saw a new heaven and a new earth: for the first heaven and the first earth were passed away: and there was no more sea. And I John saw the holy city, new Jerusalem, coming down from God out of heaven, prepared as a bride adorned for her husband. And I heard a great voice out of heaven saying, Behold, the tabernacle of God is with men, and he will dwell with them, and they shall be his people and God himself shall be with them, and be their God. And God shall wipe away all tears from their eyes; and there shall be no more death, neither sorrow, nor crying, neither shall there be any more pain: for the former things are passed away. (Revelation 21:1–4)

You believe in the rapture before the seven years of tribulation. After the tribulation, Jesus comes back.

○ For then shall be great tribulation, such as was not since the beginning of the world to this time, nor ever shall be. . . . And then shall appear the sign of the son of man in heaven: and then shall all the tribes of the earth mourn, and they shall see the Son of man coming in the clouds of heaven with power and great glory. And he shall send his angels with a great sound of a trumpet, and they shall gather together his elect from the four winds, from one end of heaven to the other. (Matthew 24:21, 30–31, 40–41)

○ Then shall two be in the field; the one shall be taken and the other left. Two women shall be grinding at the mill; the one shall be taken, and the other left. (Matthew 24:40–41)

- In a moment, in the twinkling of an eye, at the last trump: for the trumpet shall sound, and the dead shall be raised incorruptible, and we shall be changed. (1 Corinthians 15:52)
- For the Lord himself shall descend from heaven with a shout, with the voice of the archangel, and with the trump of God: and the dead in Christ shall rise first: Then we which are alive and remain shall be caught up together with them in the clouds to meet the Lord in the air: and so shall we ever be with the Lord. (1 Thessalonians 4:16–17)
- For yourselves know perfectly that the day of the Lord so cometh as a thief in the night. (1 Thessalonians 5:2)
- For he that will love life, and see good days, let him refrain his tongue from evil, and his lips that they speak no guile. Let him eschew evil, and do good: let him seek peace, and ensue it. (1 Peter 3:10–11)
- Knowing this first, that there shall come in the last days scoffers, walking after their own lusts. And saying, Where is the promise of his coming? For since the fathers fell asleep all things continue as they were from the beginning of the creation. (2 Peter 3:3–4)
- Behold, he cometh with clouds: and every eye shall see him, and they also which pierced him; and all kindreds of the earth shall wail because of him. Even so, Amen. (Revelation 1:7)
- And I said unto him, sir, thou knowest. And he said, to me, these are they which came out of great tribulation, and have washed their robes, and made them white in the blood of the Lamb. (Revelation 7:14)

Look for the signs of the end times and Jesus coming back so you don't be deceived by false messiahs. The whole world will be able to see His return.

- And Jesus went out, and departed from the temple: and his disciples came to him for to show him the buildings of the temple. And Jesus said unto them, see ye not all these things? Verily I say unto you, there shall not be left here one stone upon another, that shall not be thrown down. And as he sat upon the mount of Olives, the disciples came unto him privately, saying, tell us, when shall these things be? And what shall be the sign of thy coming, and of the end of the world? And Jesus answered and said unto them, take heed that no man deceive you. For many shall come in my name, saying, I am Christ: and shall deceive many. And ye shall hear of wars and rumors of wars: see that ye be not troubled: for all these things must come to pass but the end is not yet. For nation shall rise against nation, and kingdom against kingdom: and there shall be famines and pestilences, and earth quakes, in divers places. All these are the beginning of sorrows. Then shall they deliver you up to be afflicted, and shall kill you: and ye shall be hated of all nations for my name's sake. And then shall many be offended, and shall betray one another, and shall hate one another. And many false prophets shall rise, and shall deceive many. And because iniquity shall abound, the love of many shall wax cold. But he that shall endure unto the end, the same shall be saved. And this gospel of the kingdom shall be preached in all the world for a witness unto all nations: and then shall the end come. When ye therefore shall see the abomination of desolation, spoken of by Daniel the prophet, stand in the holy place, (whoso readeth, let him understand) Then let them which be in Judea flee into the mountains: Let him which is on the housetop not come down to take anything out of his house: Neither let him which is in the field return back to take his clothes. And woe unto them that are with child, and to them that give suck in those days! But pray ye that your flight be not in the winter, neither on the Sabbath day: For then shall be great tribulation, such as was not since the beginning of the world to this time, no, nor ever shall be. And except those days should be shortened, there should no flesh be saved: but for the elect's sake those days shall be shortened. Then if any man shall say unto you, Lo, here is Christ, or there: believe it not. For there shall arise false Christs, and false prophets, and shall show great signs and wonders: insomuch that, if it were possible, they shall deceive the very elect. Behold, I have told you before. Wherefore if they shall say unto you, Behold, he is in the desert; go not forth: behold, he is in the secret chambers; believe it not. For as the lightning cometh out of the east, shineth even unto the west: so shall also the coming of the Son of man be. For wheresoever the carcass is there will the eagles be gathered together. Immediately after the tribulation of those days shall the sun be darkened, and the moon shall not give her light, and the stars shall fall from heaven, and the powers of the heavens shall be shaken: And then shall appear the sign of the son of man in heaven: and then shall all the tribes of the earth mourn, and they shall see the Son of man coming in the clouds of heaven with power and great glory. And he shall send his angels with a great sound of a trumpet, and they shall gather together his elect from the four winds, from one end of heaven to the other. Now learn a parable of the fig tree; When his branch is yet tender and putteth forth leaves, ye know that summer is nigh: So likewise ye, when ye shall see all these things, know that it is near, even at the doors. Verily I say unto you, this generation shall not pass, till all these things be fulfilled. Heaven and earth shall pass, but my words shall not pass away. (Matthew 24:1–35)

○ And then shall they see the Son of man coming in the clouds with great power and glory. And then shall he send his angels, and shall gather together his elect from the four winds, from the uttermost part of the earth to the uttermost part of heaven. (Mark 13:26–27)

○ So being affectionately desirous of you, we were willing to have imparted unto you, not the gospel of God only, but also our own souls, because ye were dear unto us. For ye remember, brethren, our labor travail: for laboring night and day, because we would not be chargeable unto any of you, we preached unto you the gospel of God. Ye are witnesses, and God also, how holy and justly and unblamably we behaved ourselves among you that believe. As ye know how we exhorted and comforted and charged every one of you, as a father doth his children, That ye would walk worthy of God, who hath called you unto his kingdom and glory. (2 Thessalonians 2:8–12)

You believe being a Christian means having a personal relationship with God.

○ But this shall be the covenant that I will make with the house of Israel; After those day, saith the Lord, I will put my law in their inward parts, and write it in their hearts; and will be their God, and they shall be my people. And they shall teach no more every man his neighbor, and every man his brother, saying, know the Lord: for they shall all know me, from the least of them unto the greatest of them, saith the Lord:

for I will forgive their iniquity, and I will remember their sin no more. (Jeremiah 31:33–34)

○ Jesus saith unto him, Have I been so long time with you, and yet hast thou not known me, Philip? He that hath seen me hath seen the Father; and how sayest thou then, show us the Father? Believest thou not that I am in the Father, and the Father in me? The words that I speak unto you I speak not of myself: but the Father that dwelleth in me, he doeth the works. Believe me that I am in the Father, and the Father in me: or else believe me for the very works' sake. (John 14:9–11)

○ O righteous Father, the world hath not known thee: but I have known thee, and these have known that thou hast sent me. And I have declared unto them thy name, and will declare it: that the love wherewith thou hast loved me may be in them, and I in them. (John 17:25–26)

○ For this is the covenant that I will make with the house of Israel after those days, saith the Lord; I will put my laws into their mind, and write them in their hearts: and I will be to them a God, and they shall be to me a people. And they shall not teach every man his neighbor, and every man his brother, saying, know the Lord: for all shall know me, from the least to the greatest. (Hebrews 8:10–12)

You believe Jesus is the Messiah.

○ The book of the generation of Jesus Christ, the son of David, the son of Abraham. And Jacob begat Joseph the husband of Mary, of whom was born Jesus, who is called Christ. So all the generations from Abraham to David are fourteen generations; and from David until the carrying away into Babylon are fourteen generations: and from the carrying away into Babylon unto Christ are fourteen generations. Now the birth of Jesus Christ was on this wise: When as his mother Mary was espoused to Joseph, before they came together, she was found with child of the Holy Ghost. (Matthew 1:1, 16–18)

○ When Jesus came into the coasts of Caesarea Philippi, he asked his disciples, saying, whom do men say that I the Son of man am? And they said, some say that thou art John the Baptist: some, Elijah: and others, Jeremiah, or one of the prophets. He saith unto them, But whom say ye that I am? And Simon Peter answered and said, Thou are the Christ the Son of the living God. And Jesus answered and said unto him, blessed art thou, Simon Bar-jona: for flesh and blood hath not revealed it unto thee, but my Father which is in heaven. And I say also unto thee, that thou art Peter, and upon this rock I will build my church: and the gates of hell shall not prevail against it. And I will give unto thee the keys of the kingdom of heaven: and whatsoever thou shalt bind on earth shall be bound in heaven: and whatsoever thou shall loose on earth shall be loosed in heaven. (Matthew 16:13–19)

- The beginning of the gospel of Jesus Christ, the Son of God. (Mark 1:1)
- And the high priest stood up in the midst, and asked Jesus, saying, answerest thou nothing? What is it which these witness against thee? But he held his peace, and answered nothing. Again the high priest asked him, and said unto him, art though the Christ, the Son of the Blessed? And Jesus said, I am: and ye shall see the Son of man sitting on the right hand of power, and coming in the clouds of heaven. (Mark 14:60–62)
- For unto you is born this day in the city of David a Savior, which is Christ the Lord. (Luke 2:11)
- And said unto them, Thus it is written, and thus it behooved Christ to suffer, and to rise from the dead the third day. (Luke 24:46)
- But these are written, that ye might believe that Jesus is the Christ, the Son of God: and that believing ye might have life through his name. (John 20:31)
- Therefore let all the house of Israel know assuredly, that God hath made the same Jesus, whom ye have crucified, both Lord and Christ. (Acts 2:36)
- For he mightily convinced the Jews, and that publicly, showing by the Scriptures that Jesus was Christ. (Acts 18:28)
- And the seventh angel sounded: and there were great voices in heaven, saying, The kingdoms of this world are become the kingdoms of our Lord, and of his Christ; and he shall reign forever and ever. (Revelation 11:15)

You believe in the supernatural and the power of God.

○ Now the birth of Jesus Christ was on this wise: When as his mother Mary was espoused to Joseph, before they came together, she was found with child of the Holy Ghost. . . . But while he thought on these things, behold, the angel of the Lord appeared unto him in a dream, saying, Joseph thou son of David, fear not to take unto thee Mary thy wife; for that which is conceived in her is of the Holy Ghost. (Matthew 1:18, 20)

○ And these signs shall follow them that believe; In my name shall they cast out devils; they shall speak with new tongues; They shall take up serpents; and if they drink any deadly thing, it shall not hurt them; they shall lay hands on the sick, and they shall recover. (Mark 16:17–18)

○ Verily, verily, I say unto you, he that believeth on me; and greater works than these shall he do; because I go unto my Father. And whatsoever ye shall ask in my name, that will I do, that the Father may be glorified in the Son. If ye shall ask any thing in my name, I will do it. (John 14:12–14)

○ And this did she many days. But Paul, being grieved, turned and said to the spirit, I command thee in the name of Jesus Christ to come out of her. And he came out the same hour. (Acts 16:18)

○ For I am not ashamed of the gospel of Christ: for it is the power of God unto salvation to everyone that believeth; to the Jew first, and also to the Greek. (Romans 1:16)

○ For the preaching of the cross is to them that perish foolishness; but unto us which are saved it is the power of God. (1 Corinthians 1:18)

○ And if Christ be not risen, then is our preaching vain, and your faith is also vain. . . . And if Christ be not raised, your faith is vain; ye are yet in your sins. (1 Corinthians 15:14, 17)

○ Remember that Jesus Christ of the seed of David was raised from the dead according to my gospel. (2 Timothy 2:8)

○ Who his own self bare our sins in his own body on the tree, that we being dead to sins, should live unto righteousness: by whose stripes ye were healed. (1 Peter 2:24)

- Having a form of godliness, but denying the power thereof: from such turn away. (2 Timothy 3:5)

You believe you are an heir of Abraham by faith, making you the children of God or God's people.

- But he is a Jew, which is one inwardly; and circumcision is that of the heart, in the spirit, and not in the letter; whose praise is not of men, but of God. (Romans 2:29)
- For as many as are led by the Spirit of God, they are the sons of God. (Romans 8:14)
- That is, They which are the children of the flesh, these are not the children of God: but the children of the promise are counted for the seed. (Romans 9:8)
- For ye are all the children of God by faith in Christ Jesus. For as many of you as have been baptized into Christ have put on Christ. There is neither Jew nor Greek, there is neither bond nor free, there is neither male, nor female: for ye are all one in Christ Jesus. And if ye be Christ's, then are ye Abraham's seed, and heirs according to the promise. (Galatians 3:26–29)
- For in Jesus Christ neither circumcision availeth anything, nor uncircumcision: but faith which worketh by love. (Galatians 5:6)

You believe the only way to be saved, go to heaven, and have access to God is through Jesus Christ.

- For God sent not his Son into the world to condemn the world; but that the world through him might be saved. (John 3:17)
- I am the door; by me if any man enter in, he shall be saved, and shall go in and out, and find pasture. (John 10:9)
- Neither is there salvation in any other: for there is no other name under heaven given among men, whereby we must be saved. (Acts 4:12)
- In whom we have boldness and access with confidence by the faith of him. (Ephesians 3:12)
- For there is one God, and one mediator between God and men, the man Christ Jesus. (1 Timothy 2:5)

- Wherefore he is able also to save them to the uttermost that come unto God by him, seeing he ever liveth to make intercession for them. (Hebrews 7:25)

We are all equal in Christ.

- For ye are all the children of God by faith in Christ Jesus. For as many of you as have been baptized in Christ have put on Christ. There is neither Jew nor Greek, there is neither bond nor free, there is neither male nor female; for ye are all one in Christ Jesus. And if ye be Christ's then are ye Abraham's seed, and heirs according to the promise. (Galatians 3:26–29)

Salvation is a gift, not something you earn.

- Being justified freely by his grace through the redemption that is in Christ Jesus. . . . Where is boasting then? It is excluded. By what law? Of works? Nay: but by the law of faith. Therefore we conclude that a man is justified by faith without the deeds of the law. Is he the God of the Jews only? Is he not also of the Gentiles? Yes, of the Gentiles also: Seeing it is one God, which shall justify the circumcision of by faith, and uncircumcision through faith. Do we then make void the law through faith? God forbid: yea, we establish the law. (Romans 3:24, 27–31)
- For what saith the Scripture? Abraham believed God, and it was counted unto him for righteousness. . . . But to him that worketh not, but believeth on him that justifieth the ungodly, his faith is counted for righteousness. (Romans 4:3, 5)
- Let not sin therefore reign in your mortal body, that ye should obey it in the lusts thereof. Neither yield ye your members as instruments of unrighteousness unto sin: but yield yourselves unto God, as those that are alive from the dead, and your members as instruments of righteousness unto God. For sin shall not have dominion over you: for ye are not under the law, but under grace. (Romans 6:12–14)

- But now we are delivered from the law, that being dead wherein we were held: that we should serve in newness of spirit, and not in the oldness of the letter. (Romans 7:6)
- For what the law could not do, in that it was weak through the flesh God sending his own Son in the likeness of sinful flesh, and for sin, condemned sin in the flesh. That the righteousness of the law might be fulfilled in us, who walk not after the flesh, but after the Spirit. For they that are after the flesh do mind the things of the flesh; but they that are after the Spirit the things of the Spirit. (Romans 8:3–5)
- Knowing that a man is not justified by the works of the law, but by the faith of Jesus Christ, even we have believed in Jesus Christ, that we might be justified by the faith of Christ, and not by the works of the law: for by the works of the law shall no flesh be justified. (Galatians 2:16)
- He therefore that ministereth to your Spirit, and worketh miracles among you, doeth he it by the works of the law, or by the hearing of faith? ... For as many as are of the works of the law are under the curse: for it is written, Cursed is everyone that continueth not in all things which are written in the book of the law to do them. But that no man is justified by the law in the sight of God, it is evident for, the just shall live by faith. And the law is not of faith: but, the man that doeth them shall live in them. Christ hath redeemed us from the curse of the law, being made a curse for us: for it is written, cursed is everyone that hangeth on a tree. That the blessing of Abraham might come on the Gentiles through Jesus Christ; that we might receive the promise of the Spirit through faith. ... But before faith came, we were kept under the law, shut up unto the faith which should afterwards be revealed. Wherefore the law was our schoolmaster to bring us unto Christ, that we might be justified by faith. But after that faith is come, we are no longer under a schoolmaster. For ye are all the children of God by faith in Christ Jesus. (Galatians 3:5, 10–14, 23–26)
- But if ye be led of the Spirit, ye are not under the law. (Galatians 5:18)
- Even when we were dead in sins, hath quickened us together with Christ, (by grace ye are saved). ... For by grace are ye saved through faith; and that not of yourselves: it is the gift of God: Not of works, lest any man should boast. (Ephesians 2:5, 8–9)

- And be found in him, not having mine own righteousness, which is of the law, but that which is through the faith of Christ, the righteousness which is of God by faith. (Philippians 3:9)
- But after that the kindness and love of God our Savior to ward man appeared, Not by works of righteousness which we have done, but according to his mercy he saved us, by the washing of regeneration, and renewing of the Holy Ghost. (Titus 3:4–7)
- By faith Noah, being warned of God of things not seen as yet, moved with fear, prepared an ark to the saving of his house; by the which he condemned the world, and became heir of the righteousness which is by faith. (Hebrews 11:7)

Your salvation is secured from others trying to take it or to get rid of it; the only way to lose it is to jump out of His hand yourself.

- My sheep hear my voice, and I know them, and they follow me: And I give unto them eternal life; and they shall never perish, neither shall any man pluck them out of my hand. My Father, which gave them me, is greater than all; and no man is able to pluck them out of my Father's hand. (John 10:27–29)
- Who shall separate us from the love of Christ? Shall tribulation, or distress, or persecution, or famine, or nakedness, or peril, or sword? As it is written, for thy sake we are killed all the day long; we are accounted as sheep for the slaughter. Nay, in all these things we are more than conquerors through him that loved us. For I am persuaded, that neither death, nor life, nor angels, nor principalities, nor powers, nor things present, nor things to come, Nor height, nor depth, nor any other creature, shall be able to separate us from the love of God, which is in Christ Jesus our Lord. (Romans 8:35–39)
- Now unto him that is able to keep you from falling, and to present you faultless before the presence of his glory with exceeding joy, To the only wise God our Savior, be glory and majesty, dominion and power, both now and ever. Amen. (Jude 1:24–25)

You cannot say you have faith and bear no fruit; if you bear no fruit, then your faith is dead. The way to produce fruit is to stay or remain in Christ the vine.

- And now also the axe is laid unto the root of the trees: therefor every tree which bringeth not forth good fruit is hewn down, and cast into the fire. (Matthew 3:10)
- Every branch in me that beareth not fruit he taketh away: and every branch that beareth fruit, he purgeth it, that it may bring forth more fruit. (John 15:2)
- Abide in me, and I in you, As the branch cannot bear fruit of itself, except it abide in the vine; no more can ye, except ye abide in me. I am the vine, ye are the branches: He that abideth in me, and I in him, the same bringeth forth much fruit: for without me ye can do nothing ... Herein is my Father glorified, that ye bear much fruit; so shall ye be my disciples. . . . Ye have not chosen me, but I have chosen you, and ordained you, that ye should go and bring forth fruit, and that your fruit should remain: that whatsoever ye shall ask of the Father in my name, he may give it you. (John 15:4–5, 8, 16)
- What doth it profit, my brethren, though a man say he hath faith, and have not works? Can faith save him? If a brother or sister be naked, and destitute of daily food, And one of you say unto them, depart in peace, be ye warmed and filled; notwithstanding ye give them not those things which are needful to the body: what doth it profit? Even so faith, if it hath not works, is dead, being alone. Yea, a man may say, Thou hast faith, and I have works: show me thy faith without thy works, and I will show thee my faith by my works. Though believest that there is one God: thou doest well: the devils also believe, and tremble. But wilt thou know, O vain man, that faith without works is dead? Was not Abraham our father justified by works, when he had offered Isaac his son upon the altar? Seest thou how faith wrought with his works, and by works was faith made perfect? And the Scripture was fulfilled which saith, Abraham believed God, and it was imputed unto him for righteousness: and he was called the friend of God. Ye see then how that by works a man is justified, and not by faith only. Likewise also was not Rahab the harlot justified by works, when she

had received the messengers, and had sent them out another way? For as the body without the spirit is dead, so faith without works is dead also. (James 2:14–26)

You will be persecuted and suffer for your faith.

○ Blessed are they which are persecuted for righteousness' sake: for theirs is the kingdom of heaven. Blessed are ye, when men shall revile you, and persecute you, and shall say all manner of evil against you falsely, for my sake. Rejoice and be exceeding glad: for great is your reward in heaven: for so persecuted they the prophets which were before you. Ye are the salt of the earth: but if the salt have lost his savor wherewith shall it be salted? It is thenceforth good for nothing, but to be cast out, and to be trodden under foot of men. (Matthew 5:10–13)

○ And ye shall be hated of all men for my name's sake but he that endureth to the end shall be saved. But when they persecute you in this city, flee ye into another: for verily I say unto you, Ye shall not have gone over the cities of Israel, till the Son of man be come. The disciple is not above his master, nor the servant above his lord … And Jesus answered and said, Verily I say unto you, there is no man that hath left house, or brethren, or sisters, or father, or mother, or wife, or children, or land, for my sake, and the gospel's. But he shall receive a hundredfold now in this time, houses, and brethren, and sisters, and mothers, and children, and lands, with persecutions: in the world to come eternal life. But many that are first shall be last: and the last first. (Matthew 10:22–24, 29–31)

○ Then shall they deliver you up to be afflicted, and shall kill you: and ye shall be hated of all nations for my name's sake. And then shall many be offended, and shall betray one another, and shall hate one another. And many false prophets shall rise, and shall deceive many. And because iniquity shall abound, the love of many shall wax cold. But he that shall endure unto the end, the same shall be saved. And this gospel of the kingdom shall be preached in all the world for a witness unto all nations; and then shall the end come. (Matthew 24:9–14)

○ But pray ye that your flight be not in the winter, neither on the sabbath day. (John 15:20)

- For I think that God hath set forth us the apostles last, as it were appointed to death: for we are made a spectacle unto the world, and to angels, and to men. We are fools for Christ's sake, but ye are wise in Christ: we are weak, but ye are strong: ye are honorable, but we are despised. Even unto the present hour we both hunger, and thirst, and are naked, and are buffeted, and have no certain dwelling place: And labor, working with our own hands: being reviled, we bless: being persecuted, we suffer it. (1 Corinthians 4:9–13)
- We are troubled on every side, yet not distressed: we are perplexed, but not in despair; Persecuted, but not forsaken: cast down, but not destroyed; Always bearing about in the body the dying of the Lord Jesus, that the life also of Jesus might be made manifest in our body. (2 Corinthians 4:8–10)
- And he said unto me, My grace is sufficient for thee; for my strength is made perfect in weakness. Most gladly therefore will I rather glory in my infirmities, that the power of Christ may rest upon me. Therefore I take pleasure in infirmities, in reproaches, in necessities, in persecutions, in distresses for Christ's sake: for when I am weak, then am I strong. (2 Corinthians 12:9–10)
- Only let your conversation be as it becometh the gospel of Christ: that whether I come and see you, or else be absent, I may hear of your affairs, that ye stand fast in one spirit, with one mind striving together for the faith of the gospel: And in nothing terrified by your adversaries; which is to them an evident token of perdition, but to you of salvation, and that of God. For unto you it is given in the behalf of Christ, not only to believe on him, but also to suffer for his sake. (Philippians 1:27–29)
- Yea, and all that will live godly in Christ Jesus shall suffer persecution. (2 Timothy 3:12)
- And what shall I more say? For the time would fail me to tell of Gideon, and of Barak, and of Samson, and of Jephthah: of David also, and Samuel, and of the prophets: Who through faith subdued kingdoms, wrought righteousness, obtained promises, stopped the mouths of lions, quenched the violence of fire, escaped the edge of the sword, out of weakness were made strong, waxed valiant in fight, turned to fight the armies of the aliens. Women received their dead raised to

life again: and others were tortured, not accepting deliverance; that they might obtain a better resurrection. And others had trial of cruel mocking's and scourging yea, moreover of bond and imprisonment: They are stoned, they were sawn asunder, were tempted were slain with the sword: they wandered about in sheepskins and goatskins; being destitute, afflicted, tormented; And these all, having obtained a good report through faith, received not the promise. (Hebrews 11:32–38)

○ And who is he that will harm you, if ye be followers of that which is good? But and if ye suffer for righteousness sake, happy are ye; and be not afraid of their terror, neither be troubled; But sanctify the Lord God in your hearts: and be ready always to give an answer to every man that asketh you a reason of the hope that is in you with meekness and fear: Having a good conscience; that, whereas they speak evil of you, as of evildoers, they may be ashamed that falsely accuse your good conversation in Christ. (1 Peter 3:13–16)

○ Beloved, think it not strange concerning the fiery trial which is to try you, as though some strange thing happened unto you. (1 Peter 4:12)

○ If any man have an ear, let him hear. He that leadeth into captivity shall go into captivity: he that killeth with the sword must be killed with the sword. Here is the patience and the faith of the saints. (Revelation 13:9–10)

○ Fear none of those things which thou shalt suffer: behold, the devil shall cast some of you into prison, that ye may be tried; and ye shall have tribulation ten days; be though faithful unto death, and I will give thee a crown of life. (Revelation 2:10)

You believe God the Father, Jesus Christ the Son, and the Holy Spirit— all separate but one spirit.

○ Endeavoring to keep the unity of the Spirit in the bond of peace. There is one body, and one Spirit, even as ye are called in one hope of your calling; One Lord, one faith, one baptism, One God and Father of all, who is above all, and through all and in you all. (Ephesians 4:3–6)

○ For by one Spirit are we all baptized into one body, whether we be Jews or Gentiles, whether we be bond or free; and have been bond or free; and have been all made to drink into one Spirit. (1 Corinthians 12:13)

- For there are three that bear record in heaven, the Father, the Word, and the Holy Ghost: and these three are one. And there are three that bear witness in earth, and the spirit, and the water, and the blood: and these three agree in one. (1 John 5:7–8)

You believe Jesus emptied himself of God and became man on the earth.

- For what the law could not do, in that it was weak through the flesh God sending his own Son in the likeness of sinful flesh, and for sin, condemned sin in the flesh: That the righteousness of the law might be fulfilled in us, who walk not after the flesh, but after the Spirit. For they that are after the flesh do mind the things of the flesh; but they that are after the Spirit the things of the Spirit. (Romans 8:3–5)
- Let this mind be in you, which was also in Christ Jesus: Who, being in the form of God, thought it not robbery to be equal with God: But made himself of no reputation, and took upon him the form of a servant, and was made in the likeness of men: And being found in fashion as a man, He humbled himself, and became obedient unto death, even the death of the cross. (Philippians 2:5–8)
- Seeing then that we have a great high priest that is passed into the heavens, Jesus the son of God, let us hold fast our profession. For we have not a high priest which cannot be touched with the feeling of our infirmities; but was in all points tempted like as we are, yet without sin. Let us therefore come boldly unto the throne of grace, that we may obtain mercy, and find grace to help in time of need. (Hebrews 4:14–16)

You believe in the gifts of the Spirit.

- For as we have many members in one body, and all members have not the same office: So we, being many, are one body in Christ, and everyone members one of another. Having then gifts differing according to the grace that is given to us, whether prophecy, let us prophesy according to the proportion of faith: Or ministry, let us wait on our ministering: or he that teacheth, on teaching. Or he that exhorteth, on exhortation: he that giveth, let him do it with simplicity; he that ruleth, with diligence; he that showeth mercy, with cheerfulness. (Romans 12:4–8)

o   Now there are diversities of gifts, but the same Spirit. And there are differences of administrations, but the same Lord. And there are diversities of operations, but it is the same God which worketh all in all. But the manifestation of the Spirit is given to every man to profit withal. For to one is given by the Spirit the word of wisdom; to another the word of knowledge by the same Spirit; to another faith by the same Spirit; to another the gifts of healing by the same Spirit; to another the working of miracles; to another prophecy; to another discerning of spirits; to another divers kinds of tongues; to another the interpretation of tongues: But all these worketh that one and the selfsame Spirit, dividing to everyman several as he will. . . . Now ye are the body of Christ, and members in particular. And God hath set some in the church, first apostles, secondarily prophets, thirdly teachers, after that miracles, then gifts of healings, helps, governments, diversities of tongues. Are all apostles? Are all prophets? Are all teachers? Are all workers of miracles? Have all the gifts of healing? Do all speak with tongues? Do all interpret? But covet earnestly the best gifts: and yet show I unto you a more excellent way. (1 Corinthians 12:4–11, 27–31)

o   And he gave some, apostles; and some, prophets; and some, evangelists; And some, pastors and teachers; For the perfecting of the saints, for the work of the ministry, for the edifying of the body of Christ: Till we all come in the unity of the faith, and of the knowledge of the Son of God unto a perfect man, unto the measure of the stature of the fullness of Christ. (Ephesians 4:11–13)

o   God also bearing them witness, both with signs and wonders, and with divers miracles, and gifts of the Holy Ghost, according to his own will? (Hebrews 2:4)

You believe in speaking in tongues, especially after you have received the Holy Spirit.

o   And they were all filled with the Holy Ghost, and began to speak with other tongues, as the Spirit gave them utterance. (Acts 2:4) o   And they of the circumcision which believed were astonished, as many as came with Peter, because that on the Gentiles also was poured out the gift of the Holy Ghost. For they heard them speak with tongues, and magnify God. Then answered Peter, (Acts 10:45–46)

o   And when Paul had laid his hands upon them, the Holy Ghost came on them; and they spake with tongues, and prophesied. (Acts 19:6)

o   Follow after charity and desire spiritual gifts, but rather that ye may prophesy. For he that speaketh in an unknown tongue speaketh not unto men, but unto God: for no man understandeth him; howbeit in the spirit he speaketh mysteries. But he that prophesieth speaketh unto men to education, and exhortation and comfort. He that speaketh in an unknown tongue edifieth himself; but he that prophesieth edifieth the church. I would that ye all spake with tongues, but rather that ye prophesied: for greater is he that prophesieth than he that speaketh with tongues, except he interpret, that the church may receive edifying. . . . Even so ye, forasmuch as ye are zealous of spiritual gifts, seek that ye may excel to the edifying of the church. Wherefore let him that speaketh in an unknown tongue pray that he may interpret. For if I pray in an unknown tongue, my spirit prayeth, but my understanding is unfruitful. What is it then? I will pray with the spirit, and I will pray with the understanding also: I will sing with the spirit, and I will sing with the understanding also. Else when though shalt bless with the spirit, how shall he that occupieth the room of the unlearned say Amen at thy giving of thanks, seeing he understandeth not though sayest? For thou verily givest thanks well but the other is not edified. I thank my God, I speak with tongues more than ye all: Yet in the church I had rather speak five words with my understanding, that by my voice I might teach others also, than ten thousand words in an unknown tongue. . . . In the law it is written, with men of other tongues and other lips will I speak unto this people: and yet for all that will they not hear me, saith the Lord. Wherefore tongues are for a sign, not to them that believe, but to them that believe not; but prophesying serveth not for them that believe not, but for them which believe … If any man speak in an unknown tongue, let it be by two or at the most by three, and that by course; and let one interpret. But if there be no interpretation let him keep silence in the church and let him speak to himself, and to God. . . . Wherefore, brethren, covet to prophesy, and forbid not to speak with tongues. Let all things be done decently and in order. (1 Corinthians 14:1–5, 12–19, 21–22, 27–28, 39–40)

You believe the most important thing is love!

o   Though I speak with the tongues of men and of angels, and have not charity, I am become as sounding brass, or a tinkling cymbal. And though I have the gift of prophecy, and understand all mysteries, and all knowledge; and though I have all faith, so that I could remove mountains, and have not charity, I am nothing. And though I bestow all my goods to feed the poor, and though I give my body to be burned, and have not charity, it profiteth me nothing. Charity suffereth long and is kind: charity envieth not: charity vaunteth not itself, is not puffed up, Doth not behave itself unseemly, seeketh not her own, is not easily provoked, thinketh no evil; Rejoiceth not in iniquity, but rejoiceth in the truth; Beareth all things, believeth all things, hopeth all things, endureth all things. Charity never faileth; but whether there be prophecies, they shall fail whether there be tongues they shall cease; whether there be knowledge, it shall vanish away. For we know in part, and we prophesy in part. But when that which is perfect is come, then that which is in part shall be done away. When I was a child, I spake as a child, I understood as a child, I thought as a child: but when I became a man, I put away childish things. For now we see through a glass darkly; but then face to face: now I know in part; but then shall I know even as also I am known. And now abideth faith, hope, charity, these three; but the greatest of these is charity. (1 Corinthians 13:1–13)

You find your identity in Christ.

o   What? Know ye not that your body is the temple of the Holy Ghost which is in you, which ye have of God, and ye are not your own? For ye are bought with a price: therefore glorify God in your body, and in your spirit, which are God's. (1 Corinthians 6:19–20)

- Now he which establisheth us with you in Christ, and hath anointed us, is God: Who hath also sealed us, and given the earnest of the Spirit in our hearts. (2 Corinthians 1:21–22)
- Therefore if any man be in Christ, he is a new creature: old things are passed away; behold, all things are become new. (2 Corinthians 5:17)
- I am crucified with Christ; nevertheless I live; yet not I, but Christ liveth in me: and the life which I now live in the flesh I live by the faith of the Son of God, who loved me, and gave himself for me. (Galatians 2:20)
- And we have known and believed the love that God hath to us. God is love; and he that dwelleth in love dwelleth in God, and God in him. Herein is our love made perfect, that we may have boldness in the day of judgment; because as he is, so are we in the world. Herein is our love made perfect, that we may have boldness in the day of judgment; because as he is, so are we in this world. There is not fear in love; but perfect love castesth out fear: because fear hath torment. He that feareth is not made perfect in love. (1 John 4:16–18)

We are born with a sinful nature.

- What then? Are we better than they? No, in no wise: for we have before proved both Jews and Gentiles, that they are all under sin? As it is written, There is none righteous, no, not one: There is none that understandeth, there is none that seeketh after God. They are all gone out of the way, they are together become unprofitable; there is none that doeth good, no, not one. Their throat is an open sepulcher; with their tongues they have used deceit; the poison of asps is under their lips: Whose mouth is full of cursing and bitterness: Their feet are swift to shed blood: destruction and misery are in their ways: And the way of peace have they not known: There is no fear of God before their eyes. Now we know that what things soever the law saith, it saith to them who are under the law: that every mouth may be stopped, and all the world may become guilty before God. Therefore by the deeds of the law there shall no flesh be justified in his sight: for by the law is the knowledge of sin. But now the righteousness of God without the law is manifested, being witnessed by the law and the prophets;

Even the righteousness of God which is by faith of Jesus Christ unto all and upon all them that believe: for there is no difference: For all have sinned, and come short of the glory of God; Being justified freely by his grace through the redemption that is in Christ Jesus. (Romans 3:9–24)

Response

So if your sinful nature creeps up and you don't feel like going to church or reading God's Word, expect it but know that we have victory over that in Christ. (Romans 7:24-25)

You follow the greatest commandments.

○ But when the Pharisees had heard that he had put the Sadducees to silence, they were gathered together. Then one of them, which was a lawyer, asked him a question, tempting him, and saying, Master, which is the great commandment in the law? Jesus said unto him, Thou shalt love the Lord thy God with all thy heart, and with all thy soul, and with all thy mind. This is the first and great commandment. And the second is like unto it, Thou shalt love thy neighbor as thyself. On these two commandments hang all the law and the prophets. (Matthew 22:34–40)

○ And one of the scribes came, and having heard them reasoning together, and perceiving that he had answered them well, asked him, Which is the first commandment of all? And Jesus answered him, The first of all the commandments is, Hear, O Israel; The Lord our God is one Lord: And thou shall love the Lord thy God with all thy heart, and with all thy soul, and with all thy mind, and with all thy strength: this is the first commandment. And the second is like, namely this, Thou shalt love thy neighbor as thyself. There is none other commandment greater than these. And the scribe said unto him, Well, Master, thou hast said, the truth: for there is one God and there is none other but he: And to love him with all the heart and with all the understanding, and with all the soul, and with all the strength, and to love his neighbor as himself, is more than all whole burnt offerings and sacrifices. (Mark 12:28–34)

o For all the law is fulfilled in one word, even in this; Thou shalt love thy neighbor as thyself. (Galatians 5:14)

You believe in dying for your faith.

o He that loveth father or mother more than me is not worthy of me: and he that loveth son or daughter more than me is not worthy of me. (Matthew 10:37)
o For whosoever will save his life shall lose it: and whosoever will lose his life for my sake shall find it. (Matthew 16:25)
o For whosoever will save his life shall lose it: but whosoever shall lose his life for my sake and the gospel's the same shall save it. (Mark 8:35)
o And ye shall be hated of all men for my name's sake: but he that shall endure unto the end, the same shall be saved. (Mark 13:13)
o For whosoever will save his life shall lose it: but whosoever will lose his life for my sake, the same shall save it. (Luke 9:24)

You believe Christ came for freedom.

o Now the Lord is the Spirit: and where the Spirit of the Lord is, there is liberty. (2 Corinthians 3:17)
o For, brethren, ye have been called unto liberty; only use not liberty for an occasion to the flesh, but by love serve one another. (Galatians 5:13)

You believe it is a sin to get drunk, not a sin to drink.

o Let us walk honestly, as in the day; not in rioting and drunkenness, not in chambering and wantonness, not in strife and envying. (Romans 13:13)
o But now I have written unto you not to keep company, if any man that is called a brother be a fornicator or covetous, or an idolater, or a railer, or a drunkard, or an extortioner; with such a one no not to eat. (1 Corinthians 5:11)
o Know ye not that the unrighteous shall not inherit the kingdom of God? Be not deceived: neither fornicators, nor idolaters, nor adulterers,

nor effeminate, nor abusers of themselves with mankind. Nor thieves, nor covetous, nor drunkards, nor revilers, nor extortioners, shall inherit the kingdom of God. And such were some of you: but ye are washed, but ye are sanctified, but ye are justified in the name of the Lord Jesus, and by the Spirit of our God. (1 Corinthians 6:9–11)

- Now the works of the flesh are manifest, which are these; adultery, fornication, uncleanness, lasciviousness, Idolatry, witchcraft, hatred, variance, emulations, wrath, strife, seditions, heresies, Envyings, murders, drunkenness, revellings, and such like: of the which I tell you before, as I have also told you in time past, that they which do such things shall not inherit the kingdom of God. (Galatians 5:19–21)
- And be not drunk with wine, wherein is excess; but be filled with the Spirit; Speaking to yourselves in psalms and hymns and spiritual songs, singing and making melody in your heart to the Lord. (Ephesians 5:18–19)
- Therefore let us not sleep, as do others; but let us watch and be sober. For they that sleep, sleep in the night; and they that be drunken are drunken in the night. But let us, who are of the day, be sober, putting on the breastplate of faith and love; and for a helmet, the hope of salvation. (1 Thessalonians 5:6–8)
- Drink no longer water, but use a little wine for thy stomach's sake and thine often infirmities. (1 Timothy 5:23)

God is good; the devil is bad. It is that simple.

- Ye are of your father the devil, and the lusts of your father ye will do, He was a murderer from the beginning, and abode not in the truth, because there is no truth in him. When he speaketh a lie, he speaketh of his own: for he is a liar, and the father of it. (John 8:44)
- The thief cometh not, but for to steal, and to kill, and to destroy: I am come that they might have life, and that they might have it more abundantly. (John 10:10)
- Every good gift and every perfect gift is from above cometh down from the Father of lights, with whom is no variableness, neither shadow of turning. (James 1:17)

Response

With this being said, it should be obvious that things like tornadoes, storms, and death all come from the devil or sin in our body. Everything life, good, and love come from God. Yes, it says He disciplines His child and He takes care of our need to avenge by leaving room for His wrath, but He is slow to anger, abounding in love, and His mercies are new every morning. So next time there is a tornado or your aunt dies, it was not an act of God! The devil was behind it, and when we are not obeying God, it gives the devil access to do all kinds of destructive things in our lives.

You believe in being an entrepreneur.

○ For the kingdom of heaven is as a man traveling into a far country, who called his own servants, and delivered unto them his goods. And unto one he gave five talents, to another two, and to another one; to every man according to his several ability; and straightway took his journey. Then he that had received the five talents went and traded with the same, and made them other five talents. And likewise he that had received two, he also gained other two. But he that had received one went and digged in the earth, and hid his lord's money. After a long time the lord of those servants cometh, and reckoneth with them. And so he that had received five talents came and brought other five talents, saying, Lord, thou deliveredest unto me five talents: behold, I have gained beside them five talents more. His lord said unto him, well, done, thou good and faithful over a few things, I will make thee ruler over many things: enter though into the joy of the Lord. He also that had received two talents came and said, Lord, though deliveredest unto me two talents: behold, I have gained two other talents beside them. His lord said unto him, well done, good and faithful servant; thou has been faithful over a few things, I will make thee ruler over many things: enter though into the joy of thy Lord. Then he which had received the one talent came and said, Lord, I knew thee that thou art a hard man, reaping where thou hast not sown, and gathering where thou hast not strewed: And I was afraid, and went and hid thy talent in the earth: lo, there thou hast that is thine. His lord answered and said unto him, Thou wicked and slothful servant, thou knewest that I reap where I sowed not, and gather where I have not strewed: Thou oughtest therefore to have put my money to the exchangers, and then at my coming I should have received mine own with usury. Take therefore the talent from him, and give it unto him which hath ten talents. For unto every one that hath shall be given, and he shall have abundance: but from him that hath not shall be taken away even that which he hath. And cast ye the unprofitable servant into outer darkness: there shall be weeping and gnashing of teeth. (Matthew 25:14–30)

○ For ye know the grace of our Lord Jesus Christ, that, though he was rich, yet for your sakes he became poor, that ye through his poverty might be rich. (2 Corinthians 8:9)

○ Blessed be the God and Father of our Lord Jesus Christ, who had blessed us with all spiritual blessings in heavenly places in Christ. (Ephesians 1:3)

You are an overcomer in this world.

○ Behold, I give unto you power to tread on serpents and scorpions and over all the power of the enemy: and nothing shall by any means hurt you. (Luke 10:19)

○ For if by one man's offense death reigned by one; much more they which receive abundance of grace and of the gift of righteousness shall reign in life by one, Jesus Christ. (Romans 5:17)

○ Nay, in all these things we are more than conquerors through him that loved us. (Romans 8:37)

○ Ye are of God, little children, and have overcome them: because greater is he that is in you, than he that is in the world. (1 John 4:4)

○ For this is the love of God, that we keep his commandments: and his commandments are not grievous. For whatsoever is born of God over cometh the world: and this is the victory that over cometh the world, even our faith. Who is he that over cometh the world, but he that believeth that Jesus is the Son of God? (1 John 5:3–5)

- And they overcame by the blood of the Lamb, and by the word of their testimony; and they loved not their lives unto the death. (Revelation 12:11)

You are the temple of God, not the church building.

- But I say unto you, that in this place is one greater than the temple. (Matthew 12:6)
- Know ye not that ye are the temple of God, and that the Spirit of God dwelleth in you? If any man defile the temple of God, him shall God destroy; for the temple of God is holy, which temple ye are. (1 Corinthians 3:16–17)
- Flee fornication. Every sin that a man doeth is without the body: but he that committeth fornication sinneth against his own body. What? Know ye not that your body is the temple of the Holy Ghost which is in you, which ye have of God, and ye are not your own? For ye are bought with a price: therefore glorify God in your body, and in your spirit, which are God's. (1 Corinthians 6:18–20)
- And what agreement hath the temple of God with idols? For ye are the temple of the living God; as God hath said, I will dwell in them, and walk in them; and I will be their God, and they shall be my people. (2 Corinthians 6:16)
- And are built upon the foundation of the apostles and prophets, Jesus Christ himself being the chief corner stone; In whom all the building fitly framed together groweth unto a holy temple in the Lord: In whom ye also are builded together for a habitation of God through the Spirit. (Ephesians 2:20–22)

You are strangers in a foreign land, and this world is not your home, but at the same time, you are no longer a foreigner and stranger because you are a member of God's household.

- Now therefore ye are no more strangers and foreigners, but fellow citizens with the saints, and of the household of God: And are built upon the foundation of the apostles and prophets, Jesus Christ himself being the chief corner stone; In whom all the building fitly framed together groweth unto a holy temple in the Lord: In whom ye also are builded together for a habitation of God through the Spirit. (Ephesians 2:19–22)

- ○ These all died in faith, not having received the promises, but having seen them afar off, and were persuaded of them, and embraced them, and confessed that they were strangers and pilgrims on the earth. For they that say such things declare plainly that they seek a country. And truly, if they had been mindful of the country from whence they came out, they might have had opportunity to have returned. But now they desire a better country, that is, an heavenly: wherefore God is not ashamed to be called their God: for he hath prepared for them a city. (Hebrews 11:13–16)

- ○ For here have we no continuing city, but we seek one to come. (Hebrews 13:14)

- ○ Dearly beloved, I beseech you as strangers and pilgrims, abstain from fleshly lusts, which war against the soul; Having your conversation honest among the Gentiles: that, whereas they speak against you as evildoers, they may by your good works, which they shall behold, glorify God in the day of visitation. (1 Peter 2:11–12)

You are slaves to righteousness now instead of sin.

- ○ What then? Shall we sin, because we are not under the law, but under grace? God forbid. Know ye not, that to whom ye yield yourselves servants to obey, his servants ye are to whom ye obey; whether of sin unto death, or of obedience unto righteousness? But God be thanked, that ye were the servants of sin, but ye have obeyed from the heart that form of doctrine which was delivered you. Being then made free from sin, ye became the servants of righteousness. I speak after the manner of men because of the infirmity of your flesh: for as ye have yielded your members servant to uncleanness and to iniquity unto iniquity; even so now yield your members servants to righteousness unto holiness. For when ye were the servants of sin, ye were free from righteousness. What fruit had ye then in those things whereof ye are now ashamed? For the end of those things is death. But now being made free from sin, and become servants to God, ye have your fruit unto holiness, and the end everlasting life. For the wages of sin is death; but the gift of God is eternal life through Jesus Christ our Lord. (Romans 6:15–23)

The type of slave you are makes you a son, daughter, and friend of God.

○ Ye are my friends, if ye do whatsoever I command you. Henceforth I call you not servants; for the servant knoweth not what his lord doeth: but I have called you friends; for all things that I have heard of my Father I have made known unto you. (John 15:14–15)

○ For as many as are led by the Spirit of God, they are the sons of God. For ye have not received the spirit of bondage again to fear; but ye have received the Spirit of adoption, whereby we cry, Abba, Father. (Romans 8:14–15)

○ And because ye are sons, God hath sent forth the Spirit of his Son into your hearts, crying, Abba, Father. (Galatians 4:6)

○ Furthermore we have had fathers of our flesh which corrected us, and we gave them reverence: shall we not much rather be in subjection unto the Father of spirits, and live? (Hebrews 12:9)

Jesus is the same yesterday, today and forever.

○ Jesus Christ the same yesterday, and today, and forever. (Hebrews 13:8)

No one knows the day or hour Jesus will return, not even Himself. Only the Father knows.

○ But of that day and that hour knoweth no man, no, not the angels which are in heaven, neither the Son, but the Father. Take ye heed, watch and pray: for ye know not when the time is. For the Son of man is as a man taking a far journey, who left his house, and gave authority to his servants, and to every man his work, and commanded the porter to watch. Watch ye therefore: for ye know not when the master of the house cometh, at even, or at midnight, or at the cockcrowing, or in the morning. (Mark 13:32–35)

How to recognize the Spirit of God.

o   Beloved, believe not every spirit, but try the spirits whether they are of God: because many false prophets are gone out into the world. Hereby know ye the Spirit of God: Every spirit that confesseth that Jesus Christ is come in the flesh is of God: And every spirit that confesseth not that Jesus Christ is come in the flesh is not of God: and this is that spirit of antichrist, where of ye have heard that it should come; and even now already is it in the world. . . . We are of God: he that knoweth God heareth us; he that is not of God heareth not us. Hereby know we the spirit of truth, and the spirit of error. (1 John 4:1–3, 6)

What to do if someone else sins or you keep on sinning.

o   Brethren, if a man be overtaken in a fault, ye which are spiritual, restore such a one in the spirit of meekness; considering thyself, lest thou also be tempted. (Galatians 6:1)

o   Let us hold fast the profession of our faith without wavering (for he is faithful that promised;) And let us consider one another to provoke unto love and to good works; Not forsaking the assembling of ourselves together, as the manner of some is; but exhorting one another: and so much the more, as ye see the day approaching. For if we sin willfully after that we have received the knowledge of the truth, there remaineth no more sacrifice for sins, But a certain fearful looking for of judgment and fiery indignation, which shall devour the adversaries. He that despised Moses' law died without mercy under two or three witnesses: Of how much sorer punishment, suppose ye, shall he be thought worthy, who hath trodden under foot the Son of God, and hath counted the blood of the covenant, wherewith he was sanctified, an unholy thing, and hath done despite unto the Spirit of grace? For we know him that hath said, vengeance belongeth unto me, I will recompense, saith the Lord. And again, the Lord shall judge his people. It is a fearful thing to fall into the hands of the living God. (Hebrews 10:23–31)

God wants everyone to go to heaven.

○ If ye were of the world, the world would love his own: but because ye are not of the world, but I have chosen you out of the world, therefore the world hateth you. (John 15:19)

○ But we are bound to give thanks always to God for you, brethren beloved of the Lord, because God hath from the beginning chosen you to salvation through sanctification of the Spirit and belief of the truth: Whereunto he called you by our gospel, to the obtaining of the glory of our Lord Jesus Christ. (2 Thessalonians 2:13–14)

○ For this is good and acceptable in the sight of God our Savior: Who will have all men to be saved, and to come unto the knowledge of the truth. (1 Timothy 2:3–4)

○ The Lord is not slack concerning his promise, as some men count slackness; but is longsuffering to us-ward, not willing that any should perish, but that all should come to repentance. (2 Peter 3:9)

Those who respond and produce fruit have an honest and good heart.

○ And when much people were gathered together, and were come to him out of every city, he spake by a parable: A sower went out to sow his seed: and as he sowed, some fell by the way side; and it was trodden down, and the fowls of the air devoured it. And some fell upon a rock; and as soon as it was sprung up, it withered away, because it lacked moisture. And some fell among thorns; and the thorns sprang up with it, and choked it. And others fell on good ground and sprang up, and bare fruit a hundred fold. And when he had said these things, he cried, He that hath ears to hear, let him hear. And his disciples asked him, saying, What might this parable be? And he said, Unto you it is given to know the mysteries of the kingdom of God: but to others in parables; that seeing they might not see, and hearing they might not understand. Now the parable is this: The seed is the word of God. Those by the way side are they that hear; then cometh the devil, and taketh away the word out of their hearts, lest they should believe and be saved. They on the rock are they which, when they hear, receive the word with joy; and these have no root, which for a while believe, and in time of temptation fall away. And that which fell among thorns are they, which, when they have heard, go forth, and are choked with cares and riches and pleasure of this life, and bring no fruit to perfections. But that on the good ground are they, which in an honest and good heart, having heard the word, keep it, and bring forth fruit with patience. (Luke 8:4–15)

○ And with all deceivableness of unrighteousness in them that perish; because they received not the love of the truth, that they might be saved. (2 Thessalonians 2:10)

You can't love your possessions or family more than Christ.

○ He that loveth father or mother more than me is not worthy of me: and he that loveth son or daughter more than me is not worthy of me. (Matthew 10:37)

○ And every one that hath forsaken houses, or brethren, or sisters, or father, or mother, or wife, or children, or lands, for my name's sake, shall receive a hundredfold, and shall inherit everlasting life. (Matthew 19:29)

It was more important for Jesus to leave so we could receive the Holy Spirit than it was for Him to stay.

○ Nevertheless I tell you the truth; It is expedient for you that I go away: for if I go not away, the Comforter will not come unto you; but if I depart, I will send him unto you. And when he is come, he will reprove the world of sin, and of righteousness, and of judgement. (John 16:7–8)

○ How shall not the ministration of the spirit be rather glorious? (2 Corinthians 3:8)

If you don't do the good you know to do, it is sin.

○ Therefore to him that knoweth to do good, and doeth it not, to him it is sin. (James 4:17)

You believe you are not supposed to feel guilty or condemned after you ask for forgiveness for your sins.[1]

○ There is therefore now no condemnation to them which are in Christ Jesus, who walk not after the flesh, but after the Spirit. For the law of the Spirit of life in Christ Jesus hath made me free from the law of sin and death. For what the law could not do, in that it was weak through the flesh, God sending his own Son in the likeness of sinful flesh, and for sin, condemned sin in the flesh: That the righteousness of the law might be fulfilled in us, who walk not after the flesh, but after the Spirit. (Romans 8:1–4)

○ For if the ministration of condemnation be glory, much more doth the ministration of righteousness exceed in glory. (2 Corinthians 3:9)

○ Having therefore, brethren, boldness to enter into the holiest by the blood of Jesus, By a new and living way, which he hath consecrated for us, through the veil, that is to say, his flesh; And having a high priest over the house of God; Let us draw near with a true heart in full assurance of faith, having our hearts sprinkled from an evil conscience, and our bodies washed with pure water. Let us hold fast the profession of our faith without wavering; (for he is faithful that promised). (Hebrews 10:19–23)

We are dead to sin and alive to God since we are governed by the Spirit instead of the flesh.

○ Likewise reckon ye also yourselves to be dead indeed unto sin, but alive unto God through Jesus Christ our Lord. Let not sin therefore reign in your mortal body, that ye should obey it in the lusts thereof. Neither yield ye your members as instruments of unrighteousness unto sin: but yield yourselves unto God, as those that are alive from the dead, and your members as instruments of righteousness unto God. For sin shall not have dominion over you: for ye are not under the law, but under grace. (Romans 6:11–14)

○ I find then a law, that, when I would do good, evil is present with me. For I delight in the law of God after the inward man: But I see

---

[1] https://www.youtube.com/watch?v=QBRbUG-NoHg

another law in my members, warring against the law of my mind, and bringing me into captivity to the law of sin which is in my members. O wretched man that I am! Who shall deliver me from the body of this death? I thank God through Jesus Christ our Lord. So then with the mind I myself serve the law of God; but with the flesh the law of sin. (Romans 7:21–25)

○ For to be carnally minded is death; but to be spiritually minded is life and peace. . . . But ye are not in the flesh, but in the Spirit, if so be that the Spirit of God dwell in you. Now if any man have not the Spirit of Christ, he is none of his. And if Christ be in you, the body is dead because of sin; but the Spirit is life because of righteousness. But if the Spirit of him that raised up Jesus from the dead dwell in you, he that raised up Christ from the dead shall also quicken your mortal bodies by his Spirit that dwelleth in you. . . . For if ye live after the flesh, ye shall die: but if ye through the Spirit do mortify the deeds of the body, ye shall live. (Romans 8:6, 9–11, 13)

○ This I say then, Walk in the Spirit, and ye shall not fulfill the lust of the flesh. (Galatians 5:16)

○ For he that soweth to his flesh shall of the flesh reap corruption; but he that soweth to the Spirit shall of the Spirit reap life everlasting. (Galatians 6:8)

You will be without excuse when you get to heaven.

○ Enter ye in at the strait gate: for wide is the gate, and broad is the way, that leadeth to destruction, and many there be which go in thereat. (Matthew 7:13)

○ And this gospel of the kingdom shall be preached in all the world for a witness unto all nations; and then shall the end come. (Matthew 24:14)

○ If I had not come and spoken unto them, they had not had sin: but now they have no cloak for their sin. (John 15:22)

○ Because that which may be known of God is manifest in them; for God hath showed it unto them. For the invisible things of him from the creation of the world are clearly seen, being understood by the things that are made, even his eternal power and Godhead; so they are without excuse. (Romans 1:19–20)

- He that despised Moses' law died without mercy under two or three witnesses. (Hebrews 10:28)

You believe in disciplining your child.

- A whip for the horse, a bridle for the ass, and a rod for the fool's back. (Proverbs 26:3)
- He that spareth his rod hateth his son: but he that loveth him chasteneth him betimes. (Proverbs 13:24)
- Withhold not correction from the child: for if thou beatest him with the rod, he shall not die. Thou shalt beat him with the rod, and shalt deliver his soul from hell. (Proverbs 23:13-14)
- The rod and reproof give wisdom: but a child left to himself bringeth his mother to shame. (Proverbs 29:15)
- The blueness of a wound cleanseth away evil: so do stripes the inward parts of the belly. (Proverbs 20:30)
- Now no chastening for the present seemeth to be joyous, but grievous: nevertheless afterward it yieldeth the peaceable fruit of righteousness unto them which are exercised thereby. (Hebrews 12:11)

Step 5: Get Equipped to Stand Against the Devil's Schemes with the Armor of God

Imagine yourself putting it on![2]

- Finally, my brethren, be strong in the Lord, and in the power of his might. Put on the whole armor of God, that ye may be able to stand against the wiles of the devil. For we wrestle not against flesh and blood, but against principalities, against powers, against the rulers of the darkness of this world, against spiritual wickedness in high places. Wherefore take unto you the whole armor of God, that ye may be able to withstand in the evil day, and having done all, to stand. Stand therefore, having your loins girt about with truth, and having on the breastplate of righteousness; And your feet shod with the preparation of the gospel of peace; Above all, taking the shield of faith, wherewith ye shall be able to quench all the fiery darts of the wicked. And take the helmet of salvation, and the sword of the Spirit, which is the word of God: Praying always with all prayer and supplication in the Spirit, and watching thereunto with all perseverance and supplication for all saints. (Ephesians 6:10–18)
- For the weapons of our warfare are not carnal, but mighty through God to the pulling down of strongholds. (2 Corinthians 10:4)
- Now the God of peace, that brought again from the dead our Lord Jesus, that great shepherd of the sheep, through the blood of the everlasting covenant, make you perfect in every good work to do his

---

[2] http://www.godtube.com/watch/?v=7WWW7GNX

will, working in you that which is well pleasing in his sight, through Jesus Christ; to whom be glory forever and ever. Amen. (Hebrews 13:20–21)

- All Scripture is given by inspiration of God, and is profitable for doctrine, for reproof, for correction, for instruction in righteousness: That the man of God may be perfect, thoroughly furnished unto all good works. (2 Timothy 3:16–17)

Summary

Christians do not fight against people. They fight against the devil's schemes, rulers, authorities, powers of darkness, and spiritual forces of evil in the heavenly realms. The armor of God equips you to fight against and demolish strongholds of the devil. His Word says that He has equipped us to do His will and every good work.

How to Put on the Armor of God

Belt of Truth

- But have renounced the hidden things of dishonesty, not walking in craftiness, nor handling the word of God deceitfully; but by manifestation of the truth commending ourselves to every man's conscience in the sight of God. (2 Corinthians 4:2)
- By the word of truth, by the power of God, by the armor of righteousness on the right hand and on the left. (2 Corinthians 6:7)
- Wherefore putting away lying, speak every man truth with his neighbor: for we are members one of another. (Ephesians 4:25)
- My little children, let us not love in word, neither in tongue; but in deed and in truth. (1 John 3:18)

Summary

The belt of truth is choosing to speak the truth at all times.

○ Blessed are they which do hunger and thirst after righteousness: for they shall be filled. (Matthew 5:6)

○ Even the righteousness of God which is by faith of Jesus Christ unto all and upon all them that believe: for there is no difference: For all have sinned, and come short of the glory of God. (Romans 3:22–23)

○ For therein is the righteousness of God revealed from faith to faith: as it is written. The just shall live by faith. (Romans 1:17)

○ For what saith the Scripture? Abraham believed God, and it was counted unto him for righteousness. . . . But to him that worketh not, but believeth on him that justifieth the ungodly, his faith is counted for righteousness. . . . And he received the sign of circumcision, a seal of the righteousness of the faith which he had yet being uncircumcised: that he might be the father of all them that believe, though they be not circumcised; that righteousness might be imputed unto them also. (Romans 4:3, 5, 11)

○ Neither yield ye your members as instruments of unrighteousness unto sin: but yield yourselves unto God, as those that are alive from the dead, and your members as instruments of righteousness unto God. . . . Being then made free from sin, ye became the servants of righteousness. I speak after the manner of men because of the infirmity of your flesh: for as ye have yielded your members servants to uncleanness and to iniquity unto iniquity; even so now yield your members servants to righteousness unto holiness. For when ye were the servants of sin, ye were free from righteousness. (Romans 6:13, 18–20)

○ For they being ignorant of God's righteousness, and going about to establish their own righteousness, have not submitted themselves unto the righteousness of God. For Christ is the end of the law for righteousness to every one that believeth. (Romans 10:3–4)

○ But of him are ye in Christ Jesus, who of God is made unto us wisdom, and righteousness, and sanctification, and redemption. (1 Corinthians 1:30)

○ For he hath made him to be sin for us, who knew no sin; that we might be made the righteousness of God in him. (2 Corinthians 5:21)

- By the word of truth, by the power of God, by the armor of righteousness on the right hand and on the left. (2 Corinthians 6:7)
- For we through the Spirit wait for the hope of righteousness by faith. (Galatians 5:5)
- And be renewed in the spirit of your mind; And that ye put on the new man, which after God is created in righteousness and true holiness. Wherefore putting away lying, speak every man truth with his neighbor: for we are members one of another. (Ephesians 4:23–25)
- Being filled with the fruits of righteousness, which are by Jesus Christ, unto the glory and praise of God. (Philippians 1:11)
- Now no chastening for the present seemeth to be joyous, but grievous: nevertheless afterward it yieldeth the peaceable fruit of righteousness unto them which are exercised thereby. (Hebrews 12:11)
- Little children, let no man deceive you: he that doeth righteousness is righteous, even as he is righteous. (1 John 3:7)

Summary

You receive this righteousness through faith in Christ Jesus, and it is by faith you believe you are righteous through Christ. Offer yourself as an instrument of and slave to righteousness instead of sin through Christ. Christ Jesus is your righteousness, and because of it, you are the righteousness of God. You are being made new in your attitude and mind; you are putting off your old self and being created to be like God in true righteousness and holiness. Your sword and shield are weapons of righteousness, and you reap a harvest of righteousness when you sow in peace and are disciplined.

Your righteousness is also a process. First you receive it when you get saved and ask for forgiveness of your sins. It is maintained through keeping a clear conscience, and then it is made complete the day you receive your eternal life.

Feet Fitted with the Readiness That Comes from the Gospel of Peace

- To give light to them that sit in darkness and in the shadow of death, to guide our feet into the way of peace. (Luke 1:79)

- Peace I leave with you, my peace I give unto you: not as the world giveth, give I unto you. Let not your heart be troubled, neither let it be afraid. (John 14:27)
- These things I have spoken unto you, that in me ye might have peace. In the world ye shall have tribulation: but be of good cheer; I have overcome the world. (John 16:33)
- Tribulation and anguish, upon every soul of man that doeth evil, of the Jew first, and also of the Gentile; But glory, honor, and peace, to everyman that worketh good, to the Jew first and also to the Gentile: For there is no respect of persons with God. (Romans 2:9–11)
- Therefore being justified by faith, we have peace with God through our Lord Jesus Christ. (Romans 5:1)
- Recompense to no man evil for evil. Provide things honest in the sight of all men. If it be possible, as much as lieth in you, live peaceably with all men. Dearly beloved, avenge not yourselves, but rather give place unto wrath: for it is written, Vengeance is mine; I will repay, saith the Lord. (Romans 12:17–19)
- For the kingdom of God is not meat and drink; but righteousness, and peace, and joy in the Holy Ghost. . . . Let us therefore follow after the things which make for peace, and things wherewith one may edify another. (Romans 14:17, 19)
- Now the God of hope fill you with all joy and peace in believing, that ye may abound in hope, through the power of the Holy Ghost. (Romans 15:13)
- Endeavoring to keep the unity of the Spirit in the bond of peace. (Ephesians 4:3)
- Be careful for nothing but in everything by prayer and supplication with thanksgiving let your requests be made known unto God. And the peace of God, which passeth all understanding, shall keep your hearts and minds through Christ Jesus. Finally, brethren, whatsoever things are true, whatsoever things are honest, whatsoever things are just, whatsoever things are pure, whatsoever things are lovely, whatsoever things are of good report; if there be any virtue, and if there be any praise, think on these things. (Philippians 4:6–8)
- And let the peace of God rule in your hearts, to the which also ye are called in one body; and be ye thankful. (Colossians 3:15)

- Now the Lord of peace himself give you peace always by all means. The Lord be with you all. (2 Thessalonians 3:16)
- Now no chastening for the present seemeth to be joyous, but grievous: nevertheless afterward it yieldeth the peaceable fruit of righteousness unto them which are exercised thereby. (Hebrews 12:11)
- And the fruit of righteousness is sown in peace of them that make peace. (James 3:18)

Summary

Jesus came to guide our feet into the path of peace and to give you peace at all times. Also you get peace when you do good and you have peace with God through your justification by faith. You are commanded to live at peace, do things that lead to peace, and make every effort to keep the unity of the Spirit through the bond of peace. You get peace through the Holy Spirit, and you will be filled with peace as you trust Christ. You are to let the peace of God rule in your hearts and minds in Christ Jesus. Lastly, discipline in your life produces a harvest of peace. By the gospel of peace, your feet are fitted to be ready at all times.

Shield of Faith (Which You Can Extinguish All the Flaming Arrows of the Evil One)

- Then touched he their eyes, saying, According to your faith be it unto you. (Matthew 9:29)
- And he did not many mighty works there because of their unbelief. (Matthew 13:58)
- Then Jesus answered and said unto her, O woman, great is thy faith: be it unto thee even as thou wilt. And her daughter was made whole from that very hour. (Matthew 15:28)
- And Jesus said unto them, Because of your unbelief: for verily I say unto you, if ye have faith as a grain of mustard seed, ye shall say unto this mountain, Remove hence to yonder place; and it shall remove; and nothing shall be impossible unto you. (Matthew 17:20)
- Jesus answered and said unto them, verily I say unto you, if ye have faith, and doubt not, ye shall not only do this which is done to the fig

tree, but also if ye shall say unto this mountain, Be thou removed, and be thou cast into the sea; it shall be done. (Matthew 21:21)

o And he said unto her, daughter, thy faith hath made thee whole; go in peace, and be whole of thy plague. (Mark 5:34)

o And Jesus said unto him, go thy way; thy faith hath made thee whole. And immediately he received his sight, and followed Jesus in the way. (Mark 10:52)

o And Jesus answering saith unto them, have faith in God. (Mark 11:22)

o And he said to the woman, thy faith hath saved thee; go in peace. (Luke 7:50)

o And he said unto her, daughter, be of good comfort: thy faith hath made thee whole; go in peace. (Luke 8:48)

o And the Lord said, If ye had faith as a grain of mustard seed, ye might say unto this sycamore tree, be thou plucked up by the root, and be thou planted in the sea; and it should obey you ... And he said unto him, arise, go thy way: thy faith hath made thee whole. (Luke 17:6, 19)

o And Jesus said unto him, Receive thy sight: thy faith hath saved thee. (Luke 18:42)

o Wherefore, sirs, be of good cheer: for I believe God, that it shall be even as it was told me. (Acts 27:25)

o For therein is the righteousness of God revealed from faith to faith: as it is written. The just shall live by faith. (Romans 1:17)

o Where is boasting then? It is excluded. By what law? Of works? Nay: but by the law of faith. (Romans 3:27)

o For we are saved by hope: but hope that is seen is not hope: for what a man seeth, why doth he yet hope for? (Romans 8:24)

o So then faith cometh by hearing, and hearing by the word of God. (Romans 10:17)

o And he that doubteth is damned if he eat, because he eateth not of faith: for whatsoever is not of faith is sin. (Romans 14:23)

o Watch ye, stand fast in the faith, quit you like men, be strong. (1 Corinthians 16:13)

o Not for that we have dominion over your faith, but are helpers of your joy: for by faith ye stand. (2 Corinthians 1:24)

o For we walk by faith, not by sight. (2 Corinthians 5:7)

- Now faith is the substance of things hoped for, the evidence of things not seen. . . . But without faith it is impossible to please him: for he that cometh to God must believe that he is, and that he is a rewarder of them that diligently seek him. (Hebrews 11:1, 6)
- If any of you lack wisdom, let him ask of God, that giveth to all men liberally, and upbraideth not; and it shall be given him. But let him ask in faith, nothing wavering. For he that wavereth is like a wave of the sea driven with the wind and tossed. For let not that man think that he shall receive any thing of the Lord. A double minded man is unstable in all his ways. (James 1:5–8)
- Who are kept by the power of God through faith unto salvation ready to be reveal in the last time. . . . Whom having not seen, ye love; in whom, though now ye see him not, yet believing, ye rejoice with joy unspeakable and full of glory. Receiving the end of your faith, even the salvation of your souls. Of which salvation the prophets have inquired and searched diligently, who prophesied of the grace that should come unto you. (1 Peter 1:5, 8–10)
- For whatsoever is born of God overcometh the world: and this is the victory that overcometh the world, even our faith. (1 John 5:4)
- Then they took away the stone from the place where the dead was laid. And Jesus lifted up his eyes, and said, Father, I thank thee that though hast heard me. (John 11:41)
- And when he had thus spoken, he took bread, and gave thanks to God in the presence of them all: and when he had broken it, he began to eat. (Acts 27:35)
- Ye also helping together by prayer for us, that for the gift bestowed upon us by the means of many persons thanks may be given by many on our behalf. (2 Corinthians 1:11)
- Cease not to give thanks for you, making mention of you in my prayers. (Ephesians 1:16)
- Giving thanks always for all things unto God and the Father in the name of our Lord Jesus Christ. (Ephesians 5:20)
- I thank my God upon every remembrance of you, Always in every prayer of mine for you all making request with joy, For your fellowship in the gospel from the first day until now; Being confident of this very

thing, that he which hath begun a good work in you will perform it until the day of Jesus Christ. (Philippians 1:3–6)

- Be careful for nothing; but in every thing by prayer and supplication with thanksgiving let your requests be made known unto God. (Philippians 4:6)
- We give thanks to God and the Father of our Lord Jesus Christ, praying always for you, Since we heard of your faith in Christ Jesus, and of the love which ye have to all the saints. (Colossians 1:3–4)
- Continue in prayer, and watch in the same with thanksgiving. (Colossians 4:2)
- We give thanks to God always for you all, making mention of you in our prayers. (1 Thessalonians 1:2)
- I exhort therefore, that first of all, supplications, prayers, intercessions, and giving of thanks, be made for all men. (1 Timothy 2:1)
- I thank my God, making mention of thee always in my prayers. (Philemon 1:4)
- Wherefore we receiving a kingdom which cannot be moved, let us have grace, whereby we may serve God acceptably with reverence and godly fear. (Hebrews 12:28)

Summary and Response

It is by our constant faith that we are saved and healed and our prayers are granted. God cannot do miracles in your life if you do not have faith; you are supposed to have faith in God that He will do what He says.

We get our faith by hearing the Word of God. Faith is confidence in what we hope for and assurance about what we do not see. You walk by faith, not sight. It is by faith you stand firm, and anything not done in faith is sin. It is impossible to please God without faith, and our faith gives us victory to overcome the world.

In my personal experience, I found that I always pulled out or needed the shield of faith in prayer. You asked for something, yes, but after that, you are supposed to have faith that He will do it, not keep asking Him over and over again. Here are two examples:

1. One pastor—I can't remember his name—prays to God to bring revival. First, he asks God for revival, and then he begins to beg after that, pleading and crying to God, "Please bring us revival." He finally gets exasperated because it never comes and tells God that if He loved the people as much as He did, there would be revival. After he says that, he realizes something is terribly wrong. He couldn't possibly love the people more than God did!

2. This is a personal example. I pray to God to heal me. First, I ask and then continue to ask. Then I begin to plead, beg, and cry, and by the end of the second week, I doubt both God's love for me and even my salvation. I think something is terribly wrong. God loves me unconditionally with no questions asked, and I have been saved for twenty-three years and never doubted my salvation. So I go on a search at a church that gives healing classes and offers sermons on how to have faith and be healed. I learn from there how to use the shield of faith.

I included other verses in scripture where people also gave thanks every time they prayed. I have found that when a flaming arrow from the evil one comes, if you know your sword, you can put up the shield of faith. The shield of faith is thanking Him and using the scripture to back up what He said against the flaming arrow. Thank God for His Word and the things He said He would do.

An example of this would be the person begging, pleading, and crying for God to be in a church service. The arrow is God not loving you and not being there. You pull up the shield of faith and say, "Thank You, God, for what Your Word says. I will never leave you or forsake you" (Hebrews 13:5). "Thank You for being here like Your Word says, you will be."

Every time you get doubts or start to question if God is there, say, "Thank You, God. Your Word says You will never leave us nor forsake us! Also thank You, Father, for Your Word says, where two or three gather in Your name, You are there" (Matthew 18:19–20). Thank You for being here according to Your Word.

Another example would be begging, crying, and pleading for God to heal you. The arrow is saying God will never heal you and doesn't love you enough to do so. Ask Him once to heal you, and then pull out your shield of faith and stand firm on scripture that applies to your situation. Thank Him that His Word says "By His wounds you are healed" both in Isaiah 53:5 and 1 Peter 2:24. Also thank Him that His Word says, "And whosoever shall say unto this mountain be though removed and be though cast in the sea and does not doubt in his heart but believes what he said it shall be done unto him" (Mark 11:2). Command the mountain of sickness to be gone. Thank God for Mark 11:2.

When you are in faith, you are confident in what you do not see, and even defend God that He will do what He says. You get to the point that even when you go to ask, you know when you are in doubt and unbelief, which is the opposite of faith! You think you need to ask for some things. God's Word says it is already there for you, like supplying you with everything you need for every good work (2 Timothy 3:16–17).

Learn your sword by reading it and memorizing it. Then thank God for what His Word says, and every time you begin to doubt, be in unbelief about something or want to ask again. Thank Him for what His Word already says, and stand firm in your faith. You won't get sad. You will get glad and confident that by walking in faith, you will overcome the world![3]

Helmet of Salvation

○ And she shall bring forth a son, and thou shalt call his name Jesus: for he shall save his people from their sins. (Matthew 1:21)

○ And his father Zacharias was filled with the Holy Ghost, and prophesied, saying, Blessed be the Lord God of Israel; for he hath visited and redeemed his people, And hath raised up a horn of salvation for us in the house of his servant David; As he spake by the mouth of his holy prophets, which have been since the world began: That we should be saved from our enemies, and from the hand of all that hate

---

[3] For more on faith and how to walk in it, go to http://www.flcbranson.org/freedownloads-serieslist.php?category=Faith.

us; To perform the mercy promised to our fathers, and to remember his holy covenant; The oath which he swore to our father Abraham, That he would grant unto us, that we being delivered out of the hand of our enemies might serve him without fear, In holiness and righteousness before him, all the days of our life. (Luke 1:67–75)

- To give knowledge of salvation unto his people by the remission of their sins. (Luke 1:77)
- Whosoever is born of God doth not commit sin; for his seed remaineth in him: and he cannot sin, because he is born of God. (1 John 3:9)
- That we should be to the praise of his glory, who first trust in Christ. In whom ye also trust, after the gospel of your salvation: in whom also after that ye believed, ye were sealed with that Holy Spirit of promise, Which is the earnest of our inheritance until the redemption of the purchased possession, unto the praise of his glory. (Ephesians 1:12–14)
- Wherefore, my beloved, as ye have always obeyed, not as in my presence only, but now much more in my absence, work out your own salvation with fear and trembling. (Philippians 2:12)
- But let us, who are of the day, be sober, putting on the breastplate of faith and love; and for a helmet, the hope of salvation. For God hath not appointed us to wrath, but to obtain salvation by our Lord Jesus Christ. (1 Thessalonians 5:8–9)
- Therefore I endure all things for the elect's sakes, that they may also obtain the salvation which is in Christ Jesus with eternal glory. (2 Timothy 2:10)
- And that from a child thou hast known the Holy Scriptures, which are able to make thee wise unto salvation through faith which is in Christ Jesus. (2 Timothy 3:15)
- For it became him, for whom are all things, and by whom are all things, in bringing many sons unto glory, to make the captain of their salvation perfect through sufferings. (Hebrews 2:10)
- And being made perfect, he became the author of eternal salvation unto all them that obey him. (Hebrews 5:9)
- So Christ was once offered to bear the sins of many; and unto them that look for him shall he appear the second time without sin unto salvation. (Hebrews 9:28)

- Who are kept by the power of God through faith unto salvation ready to be revealed in the last time … Receiving the end of your faith, even the salvation of your souls. (1 Peter 1:5, 9)
- Beloved, when I gave all diligence to write unto you of the common salvation, it was needful for me to write unto you, and exhort you that ye should earnestly contend for the faith which was once delivered unto the saints. (Jude 1:3)
- And they said, Believe on the Lord Jesus Christ, and thou shalt be saved, and thy house. (Acts 16:31)
- Much more then, being now justified by his blood, we shall be saved from wrath through him. (Romans 5:9)
- For we are saved by hope: but hope that is seen is not hope: for what a man seeth, why doth he yet hope for? (Romans 8:24)
- For the wrath of God is revealed from heaven against all ungodliness and unrighteousness of men, who hold the truth in unrighteousness. (1 Corinthians 1:18)
- For we are unto God a sweet savor of Christ, in them that are saved, and in them that perish. (2 Corinthians 2:15)

Summary

Salvation is seen as a start, a continuation, and a finish. It starts when you get saved and believe. It continues throughout your salvation on earth with fear and trembling and finishes when you get eternal life (your souls are saved) through obedience and are saved from His wrath. Also for the continuation part, He will return to the earth a second time to save those waiting for Him. He is saving you from your sins, and this is salvation from the hand of our enemies and all them that hate us. (That is something you could pull up your shield of faith and thank God for every time you want to ask, beg, or plead to be saved from your enemies. Thank Him instead and stand firm in faith that He will do it. Be confident!)

This knowledge of your salvation comes through the forgiveness of your sins. Our hope of salvation is our helmet. God made the pioneer's (that is, your) salvation perfect through His suffering. Us being saved is the power of God!

Sword of the Spirit (Word of God)

o Wherefore lay apart all filthiness and superfluity of naughtiness, and receive with meekness the engrafted word, which is able to save your souls. (James 1:21)

o For the word of God is quick, and powerful, and sharper than any two-edged sword, piercing even to the dividing asunder of soul and spirit, and of the joints and marrow, and is a discerner of the thoughts and intents of the heart. (Hebrews 4:12)

o For this cause also thank we God without ceasing, because, when ye received the word of God which ye heard of us, ye received it not as the word of men, but as it is in truth, the word of God, which effectually worketh also in you that believe. (1 Thessalonians 2:13)

o Forbidding to marry, and commanding to abstain from meats, which God hath created to be received with thanksgiving of them which believe and know the truth. For every creature of God is good, and nothing to be refused if it be received with thanksgiving: For it is sanctified by the word of God and prayer. (1 Timothy 4:3–5)

o Of whom we have many things to say, and hard to be uttered, seeing ye are dull of hearing. For when for the time ye ought to be teachers, ye have need that one teach you again which be the first principles of the oracles of God; and are become such as have need of milk, and not of strong meat. For everyone that useth milk is unskillful in the word of righteousness: for he is a babe. But strong meat belongeth to them that are of full age, even those who by reason of use have their senses exercised to discern both good and evil. (Hebrews 5:11–14)

o And have tasted the good word of God, and the powers of the world to come. (Hebrews 6:5)

o Being born again, not of corruptible seed, but of incorruptible, by the word of God, which liveth and abideth forever. (1 Peter 1:23)

o As every man hath received the gift, even so minister the same one to another, as good stewards of the manifold grace of God. If any man speak, let him speak as the oracles of God; if any man minister, let him do it as of the ability which God giveth: that God in all things may be glorified through Jesus Christ, to who be praise and dominion forever and ever. Amen. (1 Peter 4:10–11)

- For this they willingly are ignorant of, that by the word of God the heavens were of old, and the earth standing out of the water and in the water. (2 Peter 3:5)
- I have written unto you, fathers, because ye have known him that is from the beginning. I have written unto you young men, because ye are strong, and the word of God abideth in you, and ye have overcome the wicked one. (1 John 2:14)
- His eyes were as a flame of fire, and on his head were many crowns; and he had a name written, that no man knew, but he himself. And he was clothed with a vesture dipped in blood: and his name is called The Word of God. And the armies which were in heaven followed him upon white horses, clothed in fine linen, white and clean. (Revelation 19:12–14)

You don't sin as a Christian. Christ has made every way out possible, and there is no excuse for it. Here are some verses I use regularly as a sword.

- For though we walk in the flesh, we do not war after the flesh: (For the weapons of our warfare are not carnal, but mighty through God to the pulling down of strongholds;) Casting down imaginations, and every high thing that exalteth itself against the knowledge of God, and bringing into captivity every thought to the obedience of Christ. (2 Corinthians 10:3–5)
- Thy word have I hid in mine heart, that I might not sin against thee. (Psalm 119:11)
- There hath no temptation taken you but such as is common to man: but God is faithful, who will not suffer you to be tempted above that ye are able; but will with that temptation also make a way to escape, that ye may be able to bear it. (1 Corinthians 10:13)
- And she shall bring forth a son, and thou shalt call his name JESUS: for he shall save his people from their sins. (Matthew 1:21)
- I can do all things through Christ which strengtheneth me. (Philippians 4:13)
- But thanks be to God, which giveth us the victory through our Lord Jesus Christ. (1 Corinthians 15:57)

- Whosoever abideth in him sinneth not: whosoever sinneth hath not seen him, neither known him. . . . Whosoever is born of God doth not commit sin; for his seed remaineth in him: and he cannot sin, because he is born of God. In this the children of God are manifest, and the children of the devil: whosoever doeth not righteousness is not of God, neither he that loveth not his brother. (1 John 3:6, 9–10)
- Seeing then that we have a great high priest, that is passed into the heavens, Jesus the Son of God, let us hold fast our profession. For we have not a high priest which cannot be touched with the feeling of our infirmities; but was in all points tempted like as we are, yet without sin. Let us therefore come boldly unto the throne of grace, that we may obtain mercy, and find grace to help in time of need. (Hebrews 4:14–16)
- Finally, brethren, whatsoever things are true, whatsoever things are honest, whatsoever things are just, whatsoever things are pure, whatsoever things are lovely, whatsoever thing are of good report; if there be any virtue, and if there be any praise, think on these things. (Philippians 4:8)
- Jesus said unto him, Thou shalt love the Lord thy God with all thy heart, and with all thy soul, and with all thy mind. This is the first and great commandment. And the second is like unto it, Thou shalt love thy neighbor as thyself. (Matthew 22:37–39)
- Love not the world, neither the things that are in the world. If any man love the world, the love of the Father is not in him. For all that is in the world, the lust of the flesh, and the lust of the eyes, and the pride of life, is not of the Father, but is of the world. And the world passeth away, and the lust thereof: but he that doeth the will of God abideth forever. (1 John 2:15–17)
- And we know that all things work together for good to them that love God, to them who are the called according to his purpose. . . . Nay, in all these things we are more than conquerors through him that loved us. (Romans 8:28, 37)
- And this is the confidence that we have in him, that, if we ask any thing according to his will, he heareth us; And if we know that he hear us, whatsoever we ask, we know that we have the petitions that we desired of him. (1 John 5:14–15)

- For verily I say unto you, That whosoever will say unto this mountain, Be though removed and be cast into the sea; and shall not doubt in his heart, but shall believe that those things which he saith shall come to pass; he shall have whatsoever he saith. Therefore I say unto you, What things soever ye desire when ye pray, believe that ye receive them, and ye shall have them. (Mark 11:23–24)
- And whatsoever ye do, do it heartily, as to the Lord, and not unto men. Knowing that of the Lord ye shall receive that reward of the inheritance; for ye serve the Lord Christ. (Colossians 3:23–24)
- For God hath not given us the spirit of fear; but of power, and of love, and of a sound mind. (2 Timothy 1:7)
- But if the Spirit of him that raised up Jesus from the dead dwell in you, he that raised up Christ from the dead shall also quicken your mortal bodies by his Spirit that dwelleth in you. (Romans 8:11)
- So that we may boldly say, The Lord is my helper, and I will not fear what man shall do unto me. Remember them which have the rule over you, who have spoken unto you the word of God: whose faith follow, considering the end of their conversation. Jesus Christ the same yesterday, and today, and forever. (Hebrews 13:6–8)
- And be not conformed to this world: but be ye transformed by the renewing of your mind, that ye may prove what is that good, and acceptable, and perfect will of God. (Romans 12:2)
- There is therefore now no condemnation to them which are in Christ Jesus, who walk not after the flesh, but after the Spirit. For the law of the Spirit of life in Christ Jesus hath made me free from the law of sin and death. (Romans 8:1–2)
- But the Lord is faithful, who shall establish you, and keep you from evil. (2 Thessalonians 3:3)
- Thou wilt keep him in perfect peace, whose mind is stayed on thee: because he trusteth in thee. (Isaiah 26:3)
- Forbearing one another, and forgiving one another, if any man have a quarrel against any: even as Christ forgave you, so also do ye. And above all these things put on charity, which is the bond of perfectness. And let the peace of God rule in your hearts, to the which also ye are called in one body; and be ye thankful. (Colossians 3:13-15)

Summary and Response

Humbly accept your sword, for it can save you! I encourage you to memorize your sword so you can use it and your shield as needed throughout the day. The Word of God is sharper than any two-edged sword and judges the thoughts and attitudes of the heart. The Word of God is at work in those who believe; it is through this that you were born again.

The Word of God also consecrates your food when you pray. God's Word is good, and it is by God's Word that you overcome the evil one. If anyone has the gift of speaking, they should speak as if they are speaking the very words of God.

How to Use the Sword

I included common verses that I use as a sword regularly for you to see examples. I was taught this, and we have examples in scripture of David, Paul, and so forth, who personalized God's Word. You personalize a verse and pull it out to fight against the schemes of the devil. For example, in the Old Testament, when you did the act of sin is when you were guilty of sin, but in the New Testament, it steps it up a notch when you think the thought you have sinned (Matthew 5:27). So you take every thought captive to the obedience of Christ, according to 2 Corinthians 10:5. So when you have an impure thought, you say, "I take that thought captive to the obedience of Christ." Thus, you have used your sword and gotten rid of the thought.

Another example would be 1 Corinthians 10:13, when the devil tells you that this temptation is too hard for you to bear and that no one else on the planet has ever experienced this type of temptation. "No temptation has overtaken you except what is common to mankind. And God is faithful; he will not let you be tempted beyond what you can bear. But when you are tempted, he will also provide a way out so that you can endure it." To help reinforce this you can imagine yourself doing it as you say it. It will give you a visual that will help.

But God is faithful. He will not allow you to be tempted more than what you are able to bear. But with this temptation, also make a way to escape so you will be able to bear it. Pull out this verse and your sword, and personalize it by saying, "There is no temptation taken me, but such is as common to man. But God is faithful, who will not allow me to be tempted above what I am able to bear, but will with that temptation also make a way to escape so I may be able to bear it."

Also, when you feel like you can't do something or you have no strength, you can pull out Philippians 4:13 and tell the devil to his face that you can do all things through Christ who strengthens you. "But thanks be to God! He gives us the victory through our Lord Jesus Christ" (1 Corinthians 15:57).

Here are some other verses to personalize. Philippians 4:8 reads, "Finally, brothers and sisters, whatever is true, whatever is noble, whatever is right, whatever is pure, whatever is lovely, whatever is admirable—if anything is excellent or praiseworthy—think about such things." I will indeed think about such things. It is especially important to quote that one if you are having unlovely thoughts.

Also I will love the Lord my God with all my heart, soul, and mind, for this is the first and greatest commandment. The second is like it. Love your neighbor as yourself. And "Do not love the world or anything in the world. If anyone loves the world, love for the Father is not in them. For everything in the world—the lust of the flesh, the lust of the eyes, and the pride of life—comes not from the Father but from the world. The world and its desires pass away, but whoever does the will of God lives forever" (1 John 2:15–17). Pull out your sword and quote these if you are tempted to or are loving the world.

Again, you are at work, not wanting to be there or having a bad attitude about working for a yucky boss. Colossians 3:23 says, "And whatsoever ye do, do it heartily, as to the Lord, and not unto men. As a sword: Whatsoever I do, I do it heartily, as to the Lord, and not as unto men."

Lastly, 2 Timothy 1:7 reads, "For God hath not given us the spirit of fear; but of power, and of love, and of a sound mind." Personalize it and use your sword when you are fearful. God has not given me a spirit of fear but of power, love, and a sound mind.

Shield and Sword

Sometimes you need to pull out the shield to deflect doubt and unbelief and then pull out your sword to fight against the rulers, the authorities, the powers of this dark world, and the spiritual forces of evil in the heavenly realms. For example, the shield and sword. Thank You, Father God. Your Word says in 1 John 5:14–15 that if I ask anything according to Your will, You hear me. And if I know You hear me, then I know I have what I ask of You. Thank You for that verse, and thank You for answering my prayers.

Again, the fiery dart says that everything is not going to work out all right, including doubt and unbelief. The shield and sword says, "Thank You, Father God, for Romans 8:28, which says all things work out for good for them that love God and are called according to His purposes. I love God and am called according to His purposes. Thank You, Lord, that this verse applies to me.

In the last example, another fiery dart is coming at you of condemnation and guilt for a sin you have committed but have already asked forgiveness for. Pull out your shield and sword and say, "Thank You, Father God, for Romans 8:1–2. Thank You that there is no condemnation for those who are in Christ Jesus, for the law of the Spirit of life in Christ Jesus has set you free from the law of sin and death. There is no condemnation for me because I am in Christ Jesus. The law of the Spirit of life in Christ Jesus has set me free from the law of sin and death. Thank You, Lord, for that. Thank You that in You the guilt and condemnation is gone and I don't have to sin anymore."

Step 6: Follow His Commands

If you love me, you will obey me.

○ But he that entereth in by the door is the shepherd of the sheep. To him the porter openeth; and the sheep hear his voice: and he calleth his own sheep by name, and leadeth them out. And when he putteth forth his own sheep, he goeth before them, and the sheep follow him: for they know his voice. (John 10:2–4)

○ Jesus answered and said unto him, If a man love me, he will keep my word: and my Father will love him, and we will come unto him, and make our abode with him. He that loveth me not keepeth not my sayings: and the word which ye hear is not mine, but the Father's which sent me. (John 14:23–24)

○ Ye are my friends, if ye do whatsoever I command you. Henceforth I call you not servants; for the servant knoweth not what his lord doeth: but I have called you friends; for all things that I have heard of my Father I have made known unto you. (John 15:14–15)

○ And hereby we do know that we know him, if we keep his commandments. He that saith, I know him, and keepeth not his commandments, is a liar, and the truth is not in him. But whoso keepeth his word, in him verily is the love of God perfected: hereby know we that we are in him. He that saith he abideth in him ought himself also so to walk, even as he walked. (1 John 2:3–6)

○ For this is the love of God, that we keep his commandments: and his commandments are not grievous. (1 John 5:3)

Do not forsake the assembling of yourselves together.

o   And let us consider one another to provoke unto love and to good works: Not forsaking the assembling of ourselves together, as the manner of some is; but exhorting one another: and so much the more, as ye see the day approaching. (Hebrews 10:24–25)

Pray continuously.

o   Rejoice evermore. Pray without ceasing. In everything give thanks for this is the will of God in Christ Jesus concerning you. (1 Thessalonians 5:16–18)
o   Rejoicing in hope; patient in tribulation; continuing instant in prayer. (Romans 12:12)

Here is a list of things not to do.

o   The night is far spent, the day is at hand: let us therefore cast off the works of darkness and let us put on the armor of light. Let us walk honestly, as in the day; not in rioting and drunkenness, not in chambering and wantonness, not in strife and envying. But put ye on the Lord Jesus Christ, and make not provision for the flesh, to fulfill the lust thereof. (Romans 13:12–14)
o   Know ye not that the unrighteous shall not inherit the kingdom of God? Be not deceived: neither fornicators, nor idolaters, nor adulterers, nor effeminate, nor abusers of themselves with mankind, nor thieves, nor covetous, nor drunkards, nor revilers, nor extortioners, shall inherit the kingdom of God. And such were some of you: but ye are washed, but ye are sanctified, but ye are justified in the name of the Lord Jesus, and by the Spirit of God. (1 Corinthians 6:9–11)
o   This I say then, Walk in the Spirit, and ye shall not fulfill the lust of the flesh. For the flesh lusteth against the Spirit, and the Spirit against the flesh: and these are contrary the one to the other: so that ye cannot do the things that ye would. But if ye be led of the Spirit, ye are not under the law. Now the work of the flesh are manifest, which are these; adultery, fornication, uncleanness, lasciviousness, idolatry, witchcraft, hatred, variance, emulations, wrath, strife, seditions,

heresies, Envyings, murders, drunkenness, revellings, and such like: of the which I tell you before, as I have also told you in time past, that they which do such things shall not inherit the kingdom of God. (Galatians 5:16–21)

o Let all bitterness, and wrath, and anger, and clamor, and evil speaking, be put away from you, with all malice. And be ye kind one to another, tenderhearted, forgiving one another, even as God for Christ's sake hath forgiven you. (Ephesians 4:31–32)

o When Christ, who is our life, shall appear then shall ye also appear with him in glory. Mortify therefore your members which are upon the earth; fornication, uncleanness, inordinate affection, evil concupiscence, and covetousness, which is idolatry: For which things' sake the wrath of God cometh on the children of disobedience. . . . But now ye also put off all these; anger, wrath, malice, blasphemy, filthy communication out of your mouth. (Colossians 3:4–6, 8)

o Forasmuch then as Christ hath suffered for us in the flesh, arm yourselves likewise with the same mind: for he that hath suffered in the flesh hath ceased from sin; That he no longer should live the rest of his time in the flesh to the lust of men, but to the will of God. For the time past of our life may suffice us to have wrought the will of the Gentiles, when we walked in lasciviousness, lust, excess of wine, revellings, banquetings, and abominable idolatries: Wherein they think it strange that ye run not with them to the same excess of riot, speaking evil of you. (1 Peter 4:1–4)

Here is instruction for a Christian household.

o Submitting yourselves one to another in the fear of God. Wives, submit yourselves unto your own husbands, as unto the Lord. For the husband is the head of the wife, even as Christ is the head of the church; and he is the savior of the body. Therefore as the church is subject unto Christ, so let the wives be to their own husbands in everything. Husbands, love your wives, even as Christ also loved the church, and gave himself for it; That he might sanctify and cleanse it with the washing of water by the word, That he might present it to himself a glorious church, not having spot, or wrinkle, or any such things; but that it should be holy and without blemish. So ought men to love their wives as their own bodies. He that loveth his wife loveth himself. For no man ever yet hated his own flesh; but nourisheth and cherisheth it, even as the Lord of the church: For we are members of his body, of his flesh, and of his bones. For this cause shall a man leave his father and mother, and shall be joined unto his wife, and they two shall be one flesh. This is a great mystery: but I speak concerning Christ and the church. Nevertheless let every one of you in particular so love his wife even as himself; and the wife see that she reverence her husband. (Ephesians 5:21–33)

o   Children, obey your parents in the Lord: for this is right. Honor thy father and mother; which is the first commandment with promise; That it may be well with thee, and thou mayest live long on the earth. And, ye fathers, provoke not your children to wrath: but bring them up in the nurture and admonition of the Lord. (Ephesians 6:1–4)

o   Wives, submit yourselves unto your own husbands, as it is fit in the Lord. Husbands, love your wives, and be not bitter against them. Children, obey your parents in all things: for this is well pleasing unto the Lord. Fathers, provoke not your children to anger, lest they be discouraged. (Colossians 3:18–21)

Do not make provision for the flesh to fulfil the lust thereof. Do not think about or supply the flesh with what it needs to fulfil its fleshly desire.

o   But put ye on the Lord Jesus Christ, and make not provision for the flesh, to fulfil the lusts thereof. (Romans 13:14)

Transform your mind and attitude by changing your thoughts to God's Word.

o   And be not conformed to this world: but be ye transformed by the renewing of your mind, that ye may prove what is that good, and acceptable, and perfect will of God. (Romans 12:2)

- That ye put off concerning the former conversation the old man, which is corrupt according to the deceitful lusts; And be renewed in the spirit of your mind. (Ephesians 4:22–23)
- Casting down imaginations, and every high thing that exalteth itself against the knowledge of God, and bringing into captivity every thought to the obedience of Christ. (2 Corinthians 10:5)

Don't keep on sinning.

- For though we walk in the flesh, we do not war after the flesh: (For the weapons of our warfare are not carnal, but mighty through God to the pulling down of strongholds;) Casting down imaginations and every high thing that exalteth itself against the knowledge of God, and bringing into captivity every thought to the obedience of Christ. (2 Corinthians 10:3–5)
- Thy word have I hid in mine heart, that I might not sin against thee. (Psalm 119:11)
- There hath no temptation taken you but such as is common to man: but God is faithful, who will not suffer you to be tempted above that ye are able; but with the temptation also make a way to escape, that ye may be able to bear it. (1 Corinthians 10:13)
- And she shall bring forth a son, and thou shalt call his name JESUS: for he shall save his people from their sins. (Matthew 1:21)
- I can do all things through Christ which strengtheneth me. (Philippians 4:13)
- But thanks be to God, which giveth us the victory through our Lord Jesus Christ. (1 Corinthians 15:57)
- Whosoever abideth in him sinneth not: whosoever sinneth hath not seen him, neither known him. . . . Whosoever is born of God doth not commit sin; for his seed remaineth in him: and he cannot sin, because he is born of God. In this the children of God are manifest, and the children of the devil: whosoever doeth not righteousness is not of God, neither he that loveth not his brother. (1 John 3:6, 9–10)
- Seeing then that we have a great high priest, that is passed into the heavens, Jesus the Son of God, let us hold fast our profession. For we have not a high priest which cannot be touched with the feeling of our

infirmities; but was in all point tempted like as we are, yet without sin. Let us therefore come boldly unto the throne of grace, that we may obtain mercy, and find grace to help in time of need. (Hebrews 4:14–16)

○ What shall we say then? Shall we continue in sin, that grace may abound? God forbid. How shall we, that are dead to sin, live any longer therein? Know ye not, that so many of us as were baptized into Jesus Christ were baptized into his death? Therefore we are buried with him by baptism into death: that like as Christ was raised up from the dead by the glory of the Father, even so we also should walk in newness of life. For if we have been planted together in the likeness of his death, we shall be also in the likeness of his resurrection. Knowing this, that our old man is crucified with him, that the body of sin might be destroyed, that henceforth we should not serve sin. For he that is dead is freed from sin. Now if we be dead with Christ, we believe that we shall also live with him: Knowing that Christ being raised from the dead dieth no more; death hath no more dominion over him. For in that he died, he died unto sin once: but in that he liveth, he liveth unto God. Likewise reckon ye also yourselves to be dead indeed unto sin, but alive unto God through Jesus Christ our Lord. Let not sin therefore reign in your mortal body, that ye should obey it in the lusts thereof. Neither yield ye your members as instruments of unrighteousness unto sin: but yield yourselves unto God, as those that are alive from the dead, and your members as instruments of righteousness unto God. For sin shall not have dominion over you: for ye are not under the law, but under grace. What then? Shall we sin, because we are not under the law, but under grace? God forbid. Know ye not, that to whom ye yield yourselves servant to obey, his servants ye are to whom ye obey; whether of sin unto death, or of obedience unto righteousness? But God be thanked, that ye were the servants of sin, but ye have obeyed from the heart that form of doctrine which was delivered you. Being then made free from sin, ye became the servants of righteousness. I speak after the manner of men because of the infirmity of your flesh: for as ye have yielded your members servants to uncleanness and to iniquity unto iniquity; even so now yield your members servants to righteousness unto holiness. For when ye were the servants of sin, ye were free from righteousness. What fruit had ye then in those things whereof ye are now ashamed? For the end of those things is death. But now being made free from sin, and become servants to God, ye have your fruit unto holiness, and the end everlasting life. For the wages of sin is death; but the gift of God is eternal life through Jesus Christ our Lord. (Romans 6:1–23)

Don't do revenge.

○ Ye have heard that it hath been said, Thou shalt love thy neighbor, and hate thine enemy. But I say unto you, Love your enemies, bless them that curse you, do good to them that hate you, and pray for them which despitefully use you, and persecute you; That ye may be the children of your Father which is in heaven: for he maketh his sun to rise on the evil and on the good and sendeth rain on the just and on the unjust. For if ye love them which love you, what reward have ye? Do not even the publicans the same? And if ye salute your brethren only, what do ye more than others? Do not even the publicans so? (Matthew 5:43–47)

○ Recompense to no man evil for evil. Provide things honest in the sight of all men. If it be possible, as much as lieth in you, live peaceably with all men. Dearly beloved, avenge not yourselves, but rather give place unto wrath: for it is written, Vengeance is mine; I will repay, saith the Lord. Therefore if thine enemy hunger, feed him; if he thirst, give him drink: for in so doing though shalt heap coals of fire on his head. Be not overcome by evil, but overcome evil with good. (Romans 12:17–21)

○ For we know him that hath said, vengeance belongeth unto me, I will recompense, saith the Lord. And again, the Lord shall judge his people. (Hebrews 10:30)

○ Not rendering evil for evil, or railing for railing: but contrariwise blessing; knowing that ye are thereunto called, that ye should inherit a blessing. (1 Peter 3:9)

You are free from the law, but since you are free, go ahead and uphold it, that is, the Ten Commandments and the commandments in the New Testament.

- ○ Where is boasting then? It is excluded. By what law? Of works? Nay: but by the law of faith. Therefore we conclude that a man is justified by faith without the deeds of the law. Is he the God of the Jews only? Is he not also of the Gentiles? Yes, of the Gentiles also: Seeing it is one God, which shall justify the circumcision by faith, and uncircumcision through faith. Do we then make void the law through faith? God forbid: yea, we establish the law. (Romans 3:27–31)
- ○ There is therefore now no condemnation to them which are in Christ Jesus, who walk not after the flesh, but after the Spirit. For the law of the Spirit of life in Christ Jesus hath made me free from the law of sin and death. (Romans 8:1–2)
- ○ Christ hath redeemed us from the curse of the law, being made a curse for us: for it is written, Cursed is every one that hangeth on a tree. (Galatians 3:13)
- ○ Therefore to him that knoweth to do good, and doeth it not, to him it is sin. (James 4:17)

Don't abuse grace.

- ○ What then? Shall we sin, because we are not under the law, but under grace? God forbid. (Romans 6:15)

You don't work; you don't eat!

- ○ For even when we were with you, this we commanded you, that if any would not work, neither should he eat. For we hear that there are some which walk among you disorderly working not at all, but are busybodies. Now them that are such we command and exhort by our Lord Jesus Christ, that with quietness they work, and eat their own bread. But ye, brethren, be not weary in well doing. (2 Thessalonians 3:10–13)

- But if any provide not for his own, and especially for those of his own house, he hath denied the faith, and is worse than an infidel. (1 Timothy 5:8)

Submit to governing authorities as long as it doesn't violate scripture.

- Let every soul be subject unto the higher powers. For there is no power but of God: the powers that be are ordained of God. Whosoever therefore resisteth the power, resisteth the ordinance of God: and they that resist shall receive to themselves damnation. For rulers are not a terror to good works, but to the evil. Wilt thou then not be afraid of the power? Do that which is good, and thou shalt have praise of the same: For he is the minister of God to thee for good. But if thou do that which is evil, be afraid; for he beareth not the sword in vain: for he is the minister of God a revenger to execute wrath upon him that doeth evil. Wherefore ye must needs be subject, not only for wrath, but also for conscience sake. For this cause pay ye tribute also: for they are God's minsters, attending continually upon this very thing. Render therefore to all their dues: tribute to whom tribute is due; custom to whom custom; fear to whom fear; honor to whom honor. (Romans 13:1–7)

Do the Great Commission.

- And Jesus came and spake unto them, saying, all power is given unto me in heaven and in earth. Go ye therefore, and teach all nations, baptizing them in the name of the Father, and of the Son, and of the Holy Ghost: Teaching them to observe all things whatsoever I have commanded you: and, lo, I am with you always, even unto the end of the world. Amen. (Matthew 28:18–20)
- And he said unto them, Go ye into all the world, and preach the gospel to every creature. He that believeth and is baptized shall be saved; but he that believeth not shall be damned. (Mark 16:15–16)
- And said unto them, Thus it is written, and thus it behooved Christ to suffer, and to rise from the dead the third day: And that repentance

and remission of sins should be preached in his name among all nations, beginning at Jerusalem. (Luke 24:46–47)

○ Say not ye, there are yet four months, and then cometh harvest? Behold, I say unto you, lift up your eyes, and look on the fields; for they are white already to harvest. And he that reapeth receiveth wages, and gathereth fruit unto life eternal: that both he that soweth and he that reapeth may rejoice together. And herein is that saying true, one soweth, and another reapeth. I sent you to reap that whereon ye bestowed no labor: other men labored, and ye are entered into their labors. (John 4:35–38)

○ Then said Jesus to them again, peace be unto you: as my Father hath sent me, even so send I you. (John 20:21)

○ And for me, that utterance may be given unto me, that I may open my mouth boldly, to make known the mystery of the gospel. (Ephesians 6:19)

○ And others save with fear, pulling them out of the fire. (Jude 1:23a)

Don't sin in anger or go to bed angry. Resolve it before you go to bed, or you give the devil a foothold in your life.

○ Be ye angry, and sin not: let not the sun go down upon your wrath: Neither give place to the devil. . . . And be ye kind one to another, tenderhearted, forgiving one another, even as God for Christ's sake hath forgiven you. (Ephesians 4:26–27, 32)

○ Wherefore, my beloved brethren, let every man be swift to hear, slow to speak, slow to wrath: For the wrath of man worketh not the righteousness of God. (James 1:19–20)

Only let wholesome speech come out of your mouth.

○ Let no corrupt communication proceed out of your mouth, but that which is good to the use of edifying, that it may minister grace unto the hearers. (Ephesians 4:29)

○ Neither filthiness, nor foolish talking, nor jesting, which are not convenient: but rather giving thanks. (Ephesians 5:4)

- But now ye also put off all these; anger, wrath, malice, blasphemy, filthy communication out of your mouth. (Colossians 3:8)
- Let your speech be always with grace, seasoned with salt, that ye may know how ye ought to answer every man. (Colossians 4:6)
- For in many things we offend all. If any man offend not in word, the same is a perfect man, and able also to bridle the whole body. (James 3:2)
- For he that will love life, and see good days, let him refrain his tongue from evil, and his lips that they speak no guile. (1 Peter 3:10)

Carry a weapon.

- And he said unto them, When I sent you without purse, and scrip, and shoes, lacked ye any thing? And they said, nothing. Then said, he unto them, But now, he that hath a purse, let him take it, and likewise his scrip: and he that hath no sword, let him sell his garment, and buy one. (Luke 22:35–36)

As a wife, go to your husband to ask for spiritual advice and questions.

- Let your women keep silence in the churches: for it is not permitted unto them to speak; but they are commanded to be under obedience, as also saith the law. And if they will learn any thing, let them ask their husbands at home: for it is a shame for women to speak in the church. (1 Corinthians 14:34–35)

When you come together, take communion in remembrance of our Savior.

- And as they were eating, Jesus took bread, and blessed it, and broke it, and gave it to the disciples, and said, Take, eat; this is my body. And he took the cup, and gave thanks, and gave it to them, saying, drink ye all of it; For this is my blood of the new testament, which is shed for many for the remission of sins. (Matthew 26:26–28)
- And he took bread, and gave thanks, and broke it, and gave unto them, saying, this is my body which is given for you: this do in remembrance

of me. Likewise also the cup after super, saying, this cup is the new testament in my blood, which is shed for you. (Luke 22:19–20)

○ For I have received of the Lord that which also I delivered unto you, That the Lord Jesus the same night in which he was betrayed took bread: And when he had given thanks, he broke it, and said, Take, eat: this is my body, which is broken for you: this do in remembrance of me. After the same manner also he took the cup, when he had supped, saying, This cup is the new testament in my blood: this do ye, as oft as ye drink it, in remembrance of me. For as often as ye eat this bread, and drink this cup, ye do show the Lord's death till he come. (1 Corinthians 11:23–26)

Judge yourself lest ye be judged; do it especially before communion.

○ Judge not, that ye be not judged. For with what judgment ye judge, ye shall be judged: and with what measure ye mete, it shall be measured to you again. And why behodest thou the mote that is in thy brother's eye, but considerest not the beam that is in thine own eye? Or how wilt thou say to thy brother, Let me pull out the mote out of thine eye; and, behold, a beam is in thine own eye? Thou hypocrite, first cast out the beam out of thine own eye; and then shalt thou see clearly to cast out the mote out of thy brother's eye. (Matthew 7:1–5)

○ Judge not, and ye shall not be judged: condemn not, and ye shall not be condemned: forgive, and ye shall be forgiven: Give, and it shall be given unto you; good measure, pressed down, and shaken together, and running over, shall men give into your bosom. For with the same measure that ye mete withal it shall be measured to you again. (Luke 6:37–38)

○ Wherefore whosoever shall eat this bread, and drink this cup of the Lord, unworthily, shall be guilty of the body and blood of the Lord. But let a man examine himself, and so let him eat of that bread, and drink of that cup. For he that eateth and drinketh unworthily, eateth and drinketh damnation to himself, not discerning the Lord's body. For this cause many are weak and sickly among you, and many sleep. For if we would judge ourselves, we should not be judged. But when we are judged, we are chastened of the Lord, that we should not be condemned with the world. (1 Corinthians 11:27–32)

Response

I always judge myself and ask for forgiveness of any sins I can think of and then take communion.

Pray, worship in the Holy Spirit, and be one with God.

o   But the hour cometh, and now is, when the true worshipers shall worship the Father in spirit and in truth: for the Father seeketh such to worship him. God is a Spirit: and they that worship him must worship him in spirit and in truth. (John 4:23–24)

o   Jesus answered and said unto him, if a man love me, he will keep my words: and my Father will love him, and we will come unto him and make our abode with him. (John 14:23)

o   O righteous Father, the world hath not known thee: but I have known thee, and these have known that thou hast sent me. And I have declared unto them thy name, and will declare it: that the love wherewith thou hast loved me may be in them, and I in them. 1 Corinthians 6:17

o   But he that is joined unto the Lord is one spirit. (John 17:25–26)

o   But ye, beloved, building up yourselves on your most holy faith, praying in the Holy Ghost. Keep yourselves in the love of God, looking for the mercy of our Lord Jesus Christ unto eternal life. (Jude 1:20–21)

Response

What I have learned of praying in the Spirit is what Jeanne Guyon taught from what the Lord revealed to her. Get down on your knees like you are going to pray, but instead of looking up, close your eyes and focus on your chest. Say "Jesus" slowly and quietly to yourself, focusing on your chest. Keep focusing on your chest. Say "Jesus" slowly again in about three to five second after you say it the first time. Keep praying, focusing on your chest, and saying "Jesus" slowly every five seconds until you are filled with the Spirit.

I did it, and it was the most peace I have ever experienced from head to toe. To learn more about praying in the Spirit, read Jeanne Guyon's book, *Experiencing the Depths of Jesus Christ*.

○ **But what about gray areas? Three scriptures from the Bible guide in the areas and provide information on subjects that aren't addressed in the Bible.**

"'I have the right to do anything,' you say—but not everything is beneficial. 'I have the right to do anything'—but I will not be mastered by anything" (1 Corinthians 6:12).

1. Is it helpful—physically, spiritually, and mentally?
2. Does it bring me under its power?

"Therefore, if what I eat causes my brother to fall into sin, I will never eat meat again, so that I will not cause him to fall" (1 Corinthians 8:13).

3. Does it hurt others?

"So whether you eat or drink or whatever you do, do it all for the glory of God" (1 Corinthians 10:31).

4. Does it glorify God?

Response

For more information on this study and walking in holiness, read Jerry Bridges' *The Pursuit of Holiness*.

You believe in obeying your spiritual authority.

○ Obey them that have the rule over you, and submit yourselves: for they watch for your souls, as they that must give account, that they may do it with joy, and not with grief: for that is unprofitable for you. (Hebrews 13:17)

You believe in keeping a clear conscience by asking for forgiveness for your sins.

○ And herein do I exercise myself, to have always a conscience void of offense toward God, and toward men. (Acts 24:16)

○ Holding the mystery of the faith in a pure conscience. (1 Timothy 3:9)

○ I thank God, whom I serve from my forefathers with a pure conscience, that without ceasing I have remembrance of thee in my prayers night and day. (2 Timothy 1:3)

○ How much more shall the blood of Christ, who through the eternal Spirit offered himself with out spot to God, purge your conscience from dead works to serve the living God? (Hebrews 9:14)

○ Let us draw near with a true heart in full assurance of faith, having our hearts sprinkled from an evil conscience, and our bodies washed with pure water. (Hebrews 10:22)

○ Pray for us: for we trust we have a good conscience, in all things willing to live honestly. (Hebrews 13:18)

○ And the prayer of faith shall save the sick, and the Lord shall raise him up; and if he have committed sins, they shall be forgiven him. Confess your faults one to another, and pray one for another, that ye may be healed. The effectual fervent prayer of a righteous man availeth much. (James 5:15–16)

○ Having a good conscience: that, whereas they speak evil of you, as of evildoers, they may be ashamed that falsely accuse your good conversation in Christ. . . . The like figure whereunto even baptism doth also now save us (not the putting away of the filth of the flesh, but the answer of a good conscience toward God,) by the resurrection of Jesus Christ: Who is gone into heaven, and is on the right hand of God; angels and authorities and powers being made subject unto him. (1 Peter 3:16, 21–22)

○ If we confess our sins, he is faithful and just to forgive us our sins, and to cleanse us from all unrighteousness. (1 John 1:9)

○ My little children, these things write I unto you, that ye sin not. And if any man sin, we have an advocate with the Father, Jesus Christ the righteous: And he is the propitiation for our sins: and not for ours only, but also for the sins of the whole world. (1 John 2:1–2)

You follow the New Testament or new covenant now. The new covenant is the law fulfilled. You can still glean good from the Old Testament, especially Proverbs.

○ Think not that I am come to destroy the law, or the prophets: I am not come to destroy but to fulfill. For verily I say unto you, Till heaven and earth pass, one jot or one tittle shall in no wise pass from the law, till all be fulfilled. Whosoever therefore shall break one of these least commandments, and shall teach men so, he shall be called the least in the kingdom of heaven: but whosoever shall do and teach them, the same shall be called great in the kingdom of heaven. For I say unto you, That except your righteousness shall exceed the righteousness of the scribes and Pharisees, ye shall in no case enter into the kingdom of heaven. (Matthew 5:17–20)

○ Owe no man anything, but to love one another: for he that loveth another hath fulfilled the law. (Romans 13:8)

○ But if ye be led of the Spirit, ye are not under the law. (Galatians 5:18)

○ For if the first covenant had been faultless, then should no place have been sought for the second. For finding fault with them, he saith, behold, the days come, saith the Lord, when I will make a new covenant with the house of Israel and with the house of Judah: Not according to the covenant that I made with their fathers in the day when I took them by the hand to lead them out of the land of Egypt; because they continue not in my covenant, and I regarded them not, saith the Lord. For this is the covenant that I will make with the house of Israel after those days, saith the Lord: I will put my laws into their mind, and write them in their hearts: and I will be to them a God, and they shall be to me a people. And they shall not teach every man his neighbor, and every man his brother, saying, know the Lord: for all shall know me, from the least to the greatest. For I will be merciful to their unrighteousness, and their sins and their iniquities will I remember no more. In that he saith, A new covenant, he hath made the first old. Now that which decayeth and waxeth old is ready to vanish away. (Hebrews 8:7–13)

Don't get the mark of the beast, 666, as a chip on your hand or forehead to buy, trade and sell with. You will go to hell if you do!

○ And he doeth great wonders, so that he maketh fire come down from heaven on the earth in the sight of men. And deceiveth them that dwell on the earth by the means of those miracles which he had power to do in the sight of the beast; saying to them that dwell on the earth, that they should make an image to the beast which had the wound by a sword, and did live. And he had power to give life unto the image of the beast, that the image of the beast should both speak, and cause that as many as would not worship the image of the beast should be killed. And he causeth all, both small and great, rich and poor, free and bond, to receive a mark in their right hand, or in their foreheads. And that no man might buy or sell, save he that had the mark, or the name of the beast, or the number of his name. Here is wisdom. Let him that hath understanding count the number of the beast: for it is the number of a man; and his number is six hundred threescore and six. (Revelation 13:13–18)

○ And the third angel followed them, saying with a loud voice, if any man worship the beast and his image, and receive his mark in his forehead, or in his hand, the same shall drink of the wine of the wrath of God, which is poured out without mixture into the cup of this indignation; and he shall be tormented with fire and brimstone in the presence of the holy angels, and in the presence of the Lamb: And the smoke of their torment ascendeth up forever and ever: and they have no rest day nor night, who worship the beast and his image, and whosoever receiveth the mark of his name. Here is the patience of the saints: here are they that keep the commandments of God, and the faith of Jesus. (Revelation 14:9–12)

○ And I saw thrones, and they sat upon them, and judgment was given unto them: and I saw the souls of them that were beheaded for the witness of Jesus, and for the word of God, and which had not worshiped the beast, neither his image, neither had received his mark upon their foreheads, or in their hands; and they lived and reigned with Christ a thousand years. (Revelation 20:4)

Do everything without grumbling and complaining.

○ Do all things without murmurings and disputings: That ye may be blameless and harmless, the sons of God, without rebuke, in the midst of a crooked and perverse nation, among whom ye shine as lights in the world; Holding forth the word of life; that I may rejoice in the day of Christ, that I have not run in vain, neither labored in vain. (Philippians 2:14–16)

Pay 10 percent of your income to God.

○ Honor the Lord with thy substance, and with the firstfruits of all thine increase: So shall thy barns be filled with plenty, and thy presses shall burst out with new wine. (Proverbs 3:9–10)

○ Will a man rob God? Yet ye have robbed me. But ye say, Wherein have we robbed thee? In tithes and offerings. Ye are cursed with a curse: for ye have robbed me, even this whole nation. Bring ye all the tithes into the storehouse, that there may be meat in mine house, and prove me now herewith, saith the Lord of hosts, if I will not open you the windows of heaven, and pour you out a blessing, that there shall not be room enough to receive it. And I will rebuke the devourer for your sakes, and he shall not destroy the fruits of your ground; neither shall your vine cast her fruit before the time in the field, saith the Lord of hosts. And all nations shall call you blessed: for ye shall be a delightful land, saith the Lord of hosts. (Malachi 3:8–12)

○ For this Melchisedec, king of Salem, priest of the most high God, who met Abraham returning from the slaughter of the kings, and blessed him; To whom also Abraham gave a tenth part of all; first being by interpretation King of righteousness, and after that also King of Salem, which is, King of peace; Without father, without mother, without descent, having neither beginning of days, nor end of life; but made like unto the Son of God; abideth a priest continually. Now consider how great this man was, unto whom even the patriarch Abraham gave the tenth of the spoils. And verily they that are of the sons of Levi, who receive the office of the priesthood, have a commandment to take tithes of the people according to the law, that is, of their brethren, though they come out of the loins of Abraham: But he whose descent is not counted from them received tithes of Abraham, and blessed him that had the promises. And without all contradiction the less is blessed of the better. And here men that die receive tithes; but there he receiveth them, of whom it is witnessed that he liveth. And as I may so say, Levi also, who receiveth tithes, paid tithes in Abraham. For he was yet in the loins of his father, when Melchisedec met him. If therefore perfection were by the Levitical priesthood, (for under it the people received the law,) what further need was there that another priest should rise after the order of Melchisedec, and not be called after the order of Aaron? For the priesthood being changed, there is made of necessity a change also of the law. For he of whom these things are spoken pertaineth to another tribe, of which no man gave attendance at the altar. For it is evident that our Lord sprang out of Judah; of which tribe Moses spake nothing concerning priesthood. And it is yet far more evident: for that after the similitude of Melchisedec there ariseth another priest, who is made, not after the law of a carnal commandment, but after the power of an endless life. For he testifieth, thou art a priest forever after the order of Melchisedec. For there is verily a disannulling of the commandment going before for the weakness and unprofitableness thereof. For the law made nothing perfect, but the bringing in of a better hope did; by the which we draw nigh unto God. And inasmuch as not without an oath he was made priest: (For those priests were made without an oath; but this with an oath by him that said unto him, the Lord swore and will not repent, thou are a priest forever after the order of Melchisedec:) By so much was Jesus made a surety of a better testament. And they truly were many priests, because they were not suffered to continue by reason of death: But this man, because he continueth ever, hath an unchangeable priesthood. Wherefore he is able also to save them to the uttermost that come unto God by him, seeing he ever liveth to make intercession for them. For such an high priest became us, who is holy, harmless, undefiled, separate from sinners, and made higher than the heavens; Who needeth not daily, as those high priests, to offer up sacrifice, first for his own sins, and then for the people's: for this he did once, when he offered up himself For the law maketh men high priests which have infirmity; but the word of the oath, which was since the law, maketh the Son, who is consecrated forevermore. (Hebrews 7:1–28)

- ○ Moreoever, brethren, we do you to wit of the grace of God bestowed on the churches of Macedonia; How that in a great trial of affliction the abundance of their joy and their deep poverty abounded unto the riches of their liberality. For to their power, I bear record, yea, and beyond their power they were willing of themselves; Praying us with much entreaty that we would receive the gift, and take upon us the fellowship of the ministering to the saints. And this they did, not as we hoped, but first gave their own selves to the Lord, and unto us by the will of God. (2 Corinthians 8:1–5)
- ○ But this I say, He which soweth sparingly shall reap also sparingly; and he which soweth bountifully shall reap also bountifully. Every man according as he purposeth in his heart, so let him give; not grudgingly, or of necessity: for God loveth a cheerful giver. (2 Corinthians 9:6–7)

Don't get a divorce and commands on circumcision.

- ○ But I say unto you, That whosoever shall put away his wife, saving for the cause of fornication, causeth her to commit adultery: and whosoever shall marry her that is divorced committeth adultery. (Matthew 5:32)
- ○ And unto the married I command, yet not I, but the Lord, let not the wife depart from her husband: But and if she depart, let her remain unmarried or be reconciled to her husband: and let not the husband put away his wife. But to the rest speak I, not the Lord: If any brother hath a wife that believeth not, and she be pleased to dwell with him, let him not put her away. And the woman which hath a husband that believeth not, and if he be pleased to dwell with her, let her not leave him. For the unbelieving husband is sanctified by the wife, and the unbelieving wife is sanctified by the husband: else were your children unclean; but now are they holy. But if the unbelieving depart, let him depart. A brother or a sister is not under bondage in such cases: but God hath called us to peace. For what knowest thou, O wife, whether thou shalt save thy husband? or how knowest thou, O man, whether thou shalt save thy wife? But as God hath distributed to every man,

as the Lord hath called everyone, so let him walk. And so ordain I in all churches. Is any man called being circumcised? let him not become uncircumcised. Is any called in uncircumcision? let him not be circumcised. Circumcision is nothing, and uncircumcision is nothing, but the keeping of the commandments of God. (1 Corinthians 7:10–19)

○ The wife is bound by the law as long as her husband liveth; but if her husband be dead, she is at liberty to be married to whom she will; only in the Lord. (1 Corinthians 7:39)

Step 7: How to Know If You Are a Christian or Saved

Five things confirm this:

1. **You bear fruit that everyone can see.**
2. **You keep His commandments.**
3. **The Spirit testifies with our spirit that we are God's children.**
4. **You love one another.**
5. **You have the Spirit by which you say Jesus is God's son!**

- Ye shall know them by their fruits. Do men gather grapes of thorns, or figs of thistles? Even so every good tree bringeth forth good fruit; but a corrupt tree bringeth forth evil fruit. A good tree cannot bring forth evil fruit, neither can a corrupt tree bring forth good fruit. Every tree that bringeth not forth good fruit is hewn down, and cast into the fire. Wherefore by their fruits ye shall know them. (Matthew 7:16–20)
- For a good tree bringeth not forth corrupt fruit; neither doth a corrupt tree bring forth good fruit. For every tree is known by his own fruit. For of thorns men do not gather figs, nor of a bramble bush gather they grapes. A good man out of the good treasure of his heart bringeth forth that which is good; and an evil man out of the evil treasure of his heart bringeth forth that which is evil: for of the abundance of the heart his mouth speaketh. (Luke 6:43–45)
- For the fruit of the Spirit is in all goodness and righteousness and truth. (Ephesians 5:9)
- Being filled with the fruits of righteousness, which are by Jesus Christ, unto the glory and praise of God. (Philippians 1:11)

- But the fruit of the Spirit is love, joy, peace, longsuffering, gentleness, goodness, faithfulness, meekness, temperance: against such there is no law. (Galatians 5:22–23)
- That ye might walk worthy of the Lord unto all pleasing, being fruitful in every good work, and increasing in the knowledge of God. (Colossians 1:10)
- The Spirit itself beareth witness with our spirit, that we are the children of God. (Romans 8:16)
- By this shall all men know that ye are my disciples, if ye have love one to another. (John 13:35)
- And he is the propitiation for our sins: and not for ours only, but also for the sins of the whole world. And hereby we do know that we know him, if we keep his commandments. He that saith, I know him, and keepeth not his commandments, is a liar, and the truth is not in him. But whoso keepeth his word, in him verily is the love of God perfected: hereby know we that we are in him. He that saith he abideth in him ought himself also so to walk, even as he walked. (1 John 2:2–6)
- He that loveth his brother abideth in the light, and there is none occasion of stumbling in him. . . . Let that therefore abide in you, which ye have heard from the beginning. If that which ye have heard from the beginning shall remain in you, ye also shall continue in the Son, and in the Father. (1 John 3:10, 24)
- Beloved, let us love one another: for love is of God; and everyone that loveth is born of God, and knoweth God. He that loveth not knoweth not God; for God is love. In this was manifested the love of God toward us, because that God sent his only begotten Son into the world, that we might live through him. Herein is love, not that we loved God, but that he loved us, and sent his Son to be the propitiation for our sins. Beloved, if God so loved us, we ought also to love one another. No man hath seen God at any time. If we love one another, God dwelleth in us, and his love is perfected in us. Hereby know we that we dwell in him, and he in us, because he hath given us of his Spirit. And we have seen and do testify that the Father sent the Son to be the Savior of the world. Whosoever shall confess that Jesus is the Son of God, God dwelleth in him, and he in God. And we have known and believed the love that God hath to us. God is love; and he

that dwelleth in love dwelleth in God, and God in him. Herein is our love made perfect, that we may have boldness in the day of judgment: because as he is, so are we in this world. There is no fear in love; but perfect love casteth out fear: because fear hath torment. He that feareth is not made perfect in love. We love him, because he first loved us. If a man say, I love God, and hateth his brother, he is a liar: for he that loveth not his brother whom he hath seen, how can he love God whom he hath not seen? And this commandment have we from him, That he who loveth God love his brother also. (1 John 4:7–21)

Step 8: Final Steps

Be faithful to the faith until death. Fight a good fight, and run a good race.

○ And ye shall be hated of all men for my name's sake: but he that endureth to the end shall be saved. (Matthew 10:22)

○ Moreover it is required in stewards, that a man be found faithful. (1 Corinthians 4:2)

○ And every man that striveth for the mastery is temperate in all things. Now they do it to obtain a corruptible crown; but we an incorruptible. I therefore so run, not as uncertainly; so fight I, not as one that beateth the air: But I keep under my body, and bring it into subjection: lest that by any means, when I have preached to others, I myself should be a castaway. (1 Corinthians 9:25–27)

○ By which also ye are saved, if ye keep in memory what I preached unto you, unless ye have believed in vain. (1 Corinthians 15:2)

○ Not for that we have dominion over your faith, but are helpers of your joy: for by faith ye stand. (2 Corinthians 1:24)

○ And the very God of peace sanctify you wholly; and I pray God your whole spirit and soul and body be preserved blameless unto the coming of our Lord Jesus Christ. Faithful is he that calleth you, who also will do it. (1 Thessalonians 5:23–24)

○ This charge I commit unto thee, son Timothy, according to the prophecies which went before on thee, that thou by them mightest war a good warfare. (1 Timothy 1:18)

○ Take heed unto thyself, and unto the doctrine; continue in them: for in doing this thou shalt both save thyself, and them that hear thee. (1 Timothy 4:16)

- Fight the good fight of faith, lay hold on eternal life, whereunto thou art also called, and hast professed a good profession before many witnesses. (1 Timothy 6:12)
- I have fought a good fight, I have finished my course, I have kept the faith. (2 Timothy 4:7)
- Let us hold fast the profession of our faith without wavering; (for he is faithful that promised. . . . Now the just shall live by faith: but if any man draw back, my soul shall have no pleasure in him. But we are not of them who draw back unto perdition; but of them that believe to the saving of the soul. (Hebrews 10:23, 38–39)

The last thing is to never ever undo your salvation. Don't ever! You won't go to heaven or have eternal life. You won't be free from the bondage of sin or slavery to sin, and you won't be on the side for good and God anymore against the devil.

Here are the scriptures that apply to that and there are three things to never do and one thing to always do.

- Wherefore I say unto you, all manner of sin and blasphemy shall be forgiven unto men: but the blasphemy against the Holy Ghost shall not be forgiven unto men. And whosoever speaketh a word against the Son of man, it shall be forgiven him: but whosoever speaketh against the Holy Ghost, it shall not be forgiven him, neither in this world, neither in the world to come. (Matthew 12:31–32)
- Verily I say unto you, All sins shall be forgiven unto the sons of men, and blasphemies where with soever they shall blaspheme; But he that shall blaspheme against the Holy Ghost hath never forgiveness, but is in danger of eternal damnation. (Mark 3:28–29)
- And whosoeever shall speak a word against the Son of man, it shall be forgiven him: but unto him that blasphemeth against the Holy Ghost it shall not be forgiven. (Luke 12:10)
- But whosoever shall deny me before men, him will I also deny before my Father which is in heaven. (Matthew 10:33)
- Also I say unto you, whosoever shall confess me before men, him shall the Son of man also confess before the angels of God: But he

that denieth me before men shall be denied before the angels of God. (Luke 12:8–9)

○ For if ye forgive men their trespasses, your heavenly Father will also forgive you: But if ye forgive not men their trespasses, neither will your Father forgive your trespasses. (Matthew 6:14–15)

○ Then came Peter to him, and said, Lord, how oft shall my brother sin against me, and I forgive him? Till seven times? Jesus saith unto him, I say not unto thee, until seven times: but, until seventy times seven. Therefore is the kingdom of heaven likened unto a certain king, which would take account of his servant and when he had begun to reckon, one was brought unto him, which owed him ten thousand talents. But forasmuch as he had not to pay, his lord commanded him to be sold, and his wife, and children, and all that he had, and payment to be made. The servant therefore fell down, and worshiped him, saying, Lord, have patience with me, and I will pay thee all. Then the lord of that servant was moved with compassion, and loosed him, and forgave him the debt. But the same servant went out, and found one of his fellow servants, which owed him a hundred pence: and he laid hands on him, and took him by the throat saying, pay me what thou owest. And his fellow servant fell down at his feet, and besought him, saying, have patience with me, and I will pay thee all. And he would not: but went and cast him into prison, till he should pay the debt. So when his fellow servants saw what was done, they were very sorry, and came and told unto their lord all that was done. Then his lord, after that he had called him, said unto him, O thou wicked servant, I forgave thee all that debt, because thou desiredest me: shoudest not thou also have had compassion on thy fellow servant, even as I had pity on thee? And his lord was wroth, and delivered him to the tormentors, till he should pay all that was due unto him. So likewise shall my heavenly Father do also unto you, if ye from your hearts forgive not everyone his brother their trespasses. (Matthew 18:21–35)

○ And when ye stand praying, forgive, if ye have aught against any: that your Father also which is in heaven may forgive you your trespasses. (Mark 11:25)

○ If any man defile the temple of God, him shall God destroy; for the temple of God is holy, which temple ye are. (1 Corinthians 3:17)

Response and Summary

This is the most important thing you will ever do next to getting saved. Basically, don't ever blaspheme the Holy Spirit, and don't ever deny you are a Christian before men. Always forgive, and don't destroy or kill another Christian or yourself.

If you have already done this, it says,

- For it is impossible for those who were once enlightened, and have tasted of the heavenly gift, and were made partakers of the Holy Ghost, And have tasted the good word of God, and the powers of the world to come, If they shall fall away, to renew them again unto repentance; seeing they crucify to themselves the Son of God afresh, and put him to an open shame. For the earth which drinketh in the rain that cometh oft upon it, and bringeth forth herbs meet for them by whom it is dressed, receiveth blessing from God: But that which beareth thorns and briers is rejected, and is nigh unto cursing; whose end is to be burned. (Hebrews 6:4–8)
- He that despised Moses' law died without mercy under two or three witnesses: Of how much sorer punishment, suppose ye, shall he be thought worthy, who hath trodden under foot the Son of God, and hath counted the blood of the covenant, where with he was sanctified an unholy thing, and hath done despite unto the Spirit of grace? (Hebrews 10:28–29)
- But if thine eye be evil, thy whole body shall be full of darkness. If therefore the light that is in thee be darkness, how great is that darkness! (Matthew 6:23)

Bonus

Scriptures to quote when lacking faith or struggling

- And we know that in all things God works for the good of those who love him, who have been called according to his purpose. (Romans 8:28)
- Because the one who is in you is greater than the one who is in the world. (1 John 4:4b)
- And the peace of God, which transcends all understanding, will guard your hearts and your minds in Christ Jesus. (Philippians 4:7)
- For, God has said, "I will never leave you or let you be alone." (Hebrews 13:5b)
- Now unto him that is able to keep you from falling, and to present you faultless before the presence of his glory with exceeding joy, to the only wise God our Savior, be glory and majesty, dominion and power, both now and ever. Amen. (Jude 1:24–25)
- For I know the thoughts that I think toward you, saith the Lord, thoughts of peace, and not of evil, to give you an expected end. (Jeremiah 29:11)
- When a man's ways please the Lord, he maketh even his enemies to be at peace with him. (Proverbs 16:7)

References

Hengeveld, Nick. *King James Bible.* 199 (Biblegateway.com).

Zodhiates, Spiros, ThD, and Warren Baker, DRE. *The Hebrew-Greek Key Study Bible King James Version.* Chattanooga: AMG Publishers, 1991.

Printed in the United States
By Bookmasters